Tantalizing Tagines: 99 Exquisite Recipes for Tagine Cooking

Zestful Zen Gardens Yama

:

Contents

INTRODUCTION

Welcome to Tantalizing Tagines: 99 Exquisite Recipes for Tagine Cooking! This cookbook is a celebration of the incredible tagine cooking styles of North Africa, and the vast array of flavors that can be enjoyed from this beloved cooking style.

Tagine recipes are known for their slow-cooked, intense flavors and amazing textures, making them a favorite of many home chefs around the world. Tagine cooking requires patience and attention, involving the combining of several carefully chosen ingredients, along with a variety of herbs and spices, and slowly cooking them to create a delicious combination of flavors.

This cookbook seeks to introduce readers to the world of tagines, teaching them about the different types of tagines available, the traditional flavor combinations, and the techniques involved in tagine cooking. It also lays out a range of simple, traditional recipes for beginner tagine cooks, as well as more advanced recipes for those who wish to more fully explore the possibilities of cooking with a tagine.

The recipes in this cookbook encompass the broad range of flavors and cuisines of North Africa, including Moroccan, Algerian, Tunisian, and Libyan. Recipes are broken down into several sections, including poultry, seafood, grains, vegetables, and sweets. There are also many vegetarian and vegan options for those who prefer them. Each recipe is accompanied by detailed instructions and step-by-step photographs.

With Tantalizing Tagines, readers will find all the inspiration and knowledge they need to cook delicious and delicious tagines. Whether you are a novice to tagine cooking, or an experienced chef looking for new recipes, this cookbook is for you. Grab your tagine and start cooking today!

1. Moroccan Lamb Tagine

Moroccan Lamb Tagine is a flavorful and aromatic dish that originates from Morocco. It is a slow-cooked stew made with tender lamb, a blend of spices, and a variety of vegetables. This dish is known for its rich and complex flavors, making it a favorite among food enthusiasts.
Serving: 4 servings
Preparation time: 20 minutes
Ready time: 2 hours 30 minutes

Ingredients:
- 1.5 pounds lamb shoulder, cut into chunks
- 2 tablespoons olive oil
- 1 onion, finely chopped
- 3 garlic cloves, minced
- 1 teaspoon ground cumin
- 1 teaspoon ground coriander
- 1 teaspoon ground turmeric
- 1 teaspoon ground cinnamon
- 1 teaspoon paprika
- 1 teaspoon salt
- 1/2 teaspoon black pepper
- 1/4 teaspoon cayenne pepper (optional, for heat)
- 1 cup chicken or vegetable broth
- 1 cup canned diced tomatoes
- 1 cup chopped carrots
- 1 cup chopped potatoes
- 1 cup chopped bell peppers
- 1/2 cup pitted green olives
- 1/4 cup chopped fresh cilantro, for garnish

Instructions:
1. Heat the olive oil in a large tagine or a heavy-bottomed pot over medium heat.
2. Add the lamb chunks and brown them on all sides. Remove the lamb from the pot and set aside.
3. In the same pot, add the chopped onion and minced garlic. Sauté until the onion becomes translucent and fragrant.

4. Add the ground cumin, coriander, turmeric, cinnamon, paprika, salt, black pepper, and cayenne pepper (if using). Stir well to coat the onions and garlic with the spices.
5. Return the browned lamb to the pot and mix it with the onion and spice mixture.
6. Pour in the chicken or vegetable broth and diced tomatoes. Stir to combine.
7. Cover the pot and let the tagine simmer on low heat for 1 hour.
8. After 1 hour, add the chopped carrots, potatoes, bell peppers, and green olives to the pot. Stir well.
9. Cover the pot again and let the tagine simmer for an additional 1 hour, or until the lamb is tender and the vegetables are cooked through.
10. Taste and adjust the seasoning if needed.
11. Serve the Moroccan Lamb Tagine hot, garnished with fresh cilantro. It pairs well with couscous or crusty bread.

Nutrition information per Serving: - Calories: 420
- Fat: 20g
- Carbohydrates: 25g
- Protein: 35g
- Fiber: 6g
- Sodium: 900mg

2. Chicken and Olive Tagine

Chicken and Olive Tagine is a flavorful and aromatic Moroccan dish that combines tender chicken with a medley of spices and olives. This dish is slow-cooked in a traditional tagine pot, allowing the flavors to meld together and create a deliciously tender and savory meal. Serve this Chicken and Olive Tagine with couscous or crusty bread for a complete and satisfying meal.
Serving: 4 servings
Preparation time: 15 minutes
Ready time: 1 hour 30 minutes

Ingredients:
- 4 chicken thighs, bone-in and skin-on
- 1 onion, finely chopped

- 3 cloves of garlic, minced
- 1 teaspoon ground cumin
- 1 teaspoon ground coriander
- 1 teaspoon ground paprika
- 1 teaspoon ground turmeric
- 1/2 teaspoon ground cinnamon
- 1/2 teaspoon ground ginger
- 1/4 teaspoon cayenne pepper (optional, for heat)
- 1 cup green olives, pitted
- 1 cup chicken broth
- 2 tablespoons olive oil
- Salt and pepper to taste
- Fresh cilantro or parsley, chopped (for garnish)

Instructions:

1. In a large tagine pot or a heavy-bottomed skillet, heat the olive oil over medium heat. Add the chicken thighs, skin-side down, and cook until browned and crispy, about 5 minutes. Flip the chicken and brown the other side for an additional 5 minutes. Remove the chicken from the pot and set aside.
2. In the same pot, add the chopped onion and minced garlic. Sauté until the onion becomes translucent and fragrant, about 5 minutes.
3. Add the ground cumin, coriander, paprika, turmeric, cinnamon, ginger, and cayenne pepper (if using) to the pot. Stir well to coat the onions and garlic with the spices.
4. Return the chicken thighs to the pot, nestling them into the onion and spice mixture. Add the green olives and chicken broth. Season with salt and pepper to taste.
5. Cover the pot with a lid and reduce the heat to low. Allow the tagine to simmer for 1 hour, or until the chicken is tender and cooked through.
6. Once the chicken is cooked, remove the lid and increase the heat to medium-high. Cook for an additional 10-15 minutes, or until the sauce has thickened slightly.
7. Serve the Chicken and Olive Tagine hot, garnished with fresh cilantro or parsley. This dish pairs well with couscous or crusty bread.

Nutrition information per Serving: - Calories: 350
- Fat: 20g
- Carbohydrates: 10g
- Protein: 30g

- Fiber: 3g

3. Vegetable Tagine with Couscous

Vegetable Tagine with Couscous is a delicious and healthy dish that is packed with flavors and nutrients. This Moroccan-inspired recipe combines a variety of vegetables with aromatic spices, creating a hearty and satisfying meal. Served with fluffy couscous, this dish is perfect for a weeknight dinner or for entertaining guests.
Serving: 4 servings
Preparation time: 15 minutes
Ready time: 1 hour

Ingredients:
- 2 tablespoons olive oil
- 1 onion, diced
- 3 cloves of garlic, minced
- 1 teaspoon ground cumin
- 1 teaspoon ground coriander
- 1 teaspoon ground turmeric
- 1 teaspoon paprika
- 1/2 teaspoon ground cinnamon
- 1/4 teaspoon cayenne pepper (optional, for heat)
- 1 eggplant, diced
- 2 zucchinis, diced
- 2 carrots, sliced
- 1 red bell pepper, diced
- 1 can (400g) diced tomatoes
- 1 cup vegetable broth
- 1 cup chickpeas, cooked or canned
- Salt and pepper to taste
- Fresh cilantro or parsley, chopped (for garnish)

For the couscous:
- 1 cup couscous
- 1 cup boiling water
- 1 tablespoon olive oil
- Salt to taste

Instructions:

1. Heat the olive oil in a large pot or tagine over medium heat. Add the diced onion and minced garlic, and sauté until they become translucent and fragrant.
2. Add the ground cumin, coriander, turmeric, paprika, cinnamon, and cayenne pepper (if using) to the pot. Stir well to coat the onions and garlic with the spices.
3. Add the diced eggplant, zucchinis, carrots, and red bell pepper to the pot. Stir to combine the vegetables with the spices.
4. Pour in the diced tomatoes and vegetable broth. Bring the mixture to a simmer, then reduce the heat to low. Cover the pot and let it cook for about 45 minutes, or until the vegetables are tender.
5. Meanwhile, prepare the couscous. In a separate bowl, combine the couscous, boiling water, olive oil, and salt. Cover the bowl with a plate or plastic wrap and let it sit for 5 minutes, or until the couscous absorbs the water and becomes fluffy. Fluff the couscous with a fork before serving.
6. Once the vegetables are cooked, add the chickpeas to the pot and season with salt and pepper to taste. Stir well to combine all the Ingredients.
7. Serve the vegetable tagine over a bed of fluffy couscous. Garnish with fresh cilantro or parsley.

Nutrition information per Serving: - Calories: 320

- Fat: 8g
- Carbohydrates: 55g
- Fiber: 12g
- Protein: 10g
- Sodium: 480mg

4. Beef and Prune Tagine

Beef and Prune Tagine is a delicious and aromatic Moroccan dish that combines tender beef, sweet prunes, and a blend of warm spices. This slow-cooked stew is perfect for a cozy dinner on a chilly evening. The rich flavors and tender meat make it a crowd-pleaser that will leave everyone wanting more.

Serving: 4 servings

Preparation time: 15 minutes

Ready time: 2 hours 30 minutes

Ingredients:
- 1.5 pounds beef stew meat, cut into chunks
- 1 onion, finely chopped
- 3 cloves garlic, minced
- 1 teaspoon ground cumin
- 1 teaspoon ground coriander
- 1 teaspoon ground cinnamon
- 1/2 teaspoon ground ginger
- 1/2 teaspoon ground turmeric
- 1/4 teaspoon cayenne pepper (optional, for heat)
- 1 cup pitted prunes
- 2 cups beef broth
- 2 tablespoons olive oil
- Salt and pepper, to taste
- Fresh cilantro, for garnish

Instructions:
1. In a large pot or tagine, heat the olive oil over medium heat. Add the chopped onion and minced garlic, and sauté until the onion becomes translucent and fragrant.
2. Add the beef stew meat to the pot and brown it on all sides. This will help seal in the juices and add flavor to the dish.
3. Once the meat is browned, add the ground cumin, coriander, cinnamon, ginger, turmeric, and cayenne pepper (if using). Stir well to coat the meat and onions with the spices.
4. Pour in the beef broth and bring the mixture to a simmer. Cover the pot and let it cook on low heat for about 2 hours, or until the beef is tender and easily falls apart.
5. After 2 hours, add the pitted prunes to the pot and stir them into the stew. Let the tagine cook for an additional 30 minutes, uncovered, to allow the flavors to meld together.
6. Season with salt and pepper to taste. Serve the Beef and Prune Tagine hot, garnished with fresh cilantro. It pairs well with couscous or crusty bread.

Nutrition information:
- Calories: 380
- Fat: 14g

- Carbohydrates: 32g
- Protein: 32g
- Fiber: 4g
- Sugar: 20g
- Sodium: 600mg

Note: Nutrition information may vary depending on the specific Ingredients and brands used.

5. Fish Tagine with Chermoula Sauce

Fish Tagine with Chermoula Sauce is a delicious and flavorful Moroccan dish that combines tender fish with a tangy and aromatic sauce. This dish is perfect for seafood lovers and those who enjoy exotic flavors. The Chermoula sauce adds a burst of freshness and complements the delicate flavors of the fish. Serve this dish with couscous or crusty bread for a complete meal.

Serving: 4 servings

Preparation time: 15 minutes

Ready time: 45 minutes

Ingredients:

- 4 fish fillets (such as cod, halibut, or sea bass)
- 2 tablespoons olive oil
- 1 onion, finely chopped
- 3 garlic cloves, minced
- 1 teaspoon ground cumin
- 1 teaspoon ground coriander
- 1 teaspoon paprika
- 1/2 teaspoon ground turmeric
- 1/2 teaspoon ground cinnamon
- 1/4 teaspoon cayenne pepper (optional, for heat)
- 1 cup chopped tomatoes
- 1/4 cup chopped fresh cilantro
- 1/4 cup chopped fresh parsley
- Salt and pepper to taste

For the Chermoula Sauce:

- 1/4 cup fresh lemon juice
- 1/4 cup olive oil

- 3 garlic cloves, minced
- 1 teaspoon ground cumin
- 1 teaspoon ground coriander
- 1 teaspoon paprika
- 1/2 teaspoon ground turmeric
- 1/2 teaspoon ground cinnamon
- 1/4 teaspoon cayenne pepper (optional, for heat)
- Salt and pepper to taste

Instructions:
1. In a bowl, combine all the Ingredients for the Chermoula sauce. Mix well and set aside.
2. Preheat the oven to 375°F (190°C).
3. In a large oven-safe skillet or tagine, heat the olive oil over medium heat. Add the chopped onion and minced garlic. Sauté until the onion becomes translucent and the garlic is fragrant.
4. Add the ground cumin, ground coriander, paprika, ground turmeric, ground cinnamon, and cayenne pepper (if using) to the skillet. Stir well to coat the onions and garlic with the spices.
5. Add the chopped tomatoes, fresh cilantro, and fresh parsley to the skillet. Season with salt and pepper to taste. Cook for 5 minutes, stirring occasionally.
6. Place the fish fillets on top of the tomato mixture in the skillet. Spoon the Chermoula sauce over the fish, covering it completely.
7. Cover the skillet with a lid or aluminum foil and transfer it to the preheated oven. Bake for 25-30 minutes, or until the fish is cooked through and flakes easily with a fork.
8. Remove the skillet from the oven and let it rest for a few minutes before serving.
9. Serve the Fish Tagine with Chermoula Sauce hot, with couscous or crusty bread on the side.

Nutrition information:
- Calories: 250 per Serving: - Fat: 12g
- Carbohydrates: 8g
- Protein: 25g
- Fiber: 2g
- Sodium: 300mg

6. Moroccan Chicken Tagine with Preserved Lemons

Moroccan Chicken Tagine with Preserved Lemons is a flavorful and aromatic dish that combines tender chicken with the tangy and slightly salty taste of preserved lemons. This traditional Moroccan dish is slow-cooked in a tagine, a clay pot with a conical lid, which helps to infuse the flavors and create a deliciously tender chicken. Serve this dish with couscous or crusty bread for a complete and satisfying meal.
Serving: 4 servings
Preparation time: 15 minutes
Ready time: 1 hour 30 minutes

Ingredients:
- 4 chicken thighs, bone-in and skin-on
- 2 tablespoons olive oil
- 1 onion, finely chopped
- 3 cloves of garlic, minced
- 1 teaspoon ground cumin
- 1 teaspoon ground coriander
- 1 teaspoon ground paprika
- 1/2 teaspoon ground turmeric
- 1/2 teaspoon ground cinnamon
- 1/4 teaspoon cayenne pepper (optional, for heat)
- 2 preserved lemons, rinsed and cut into quarters
- 1 cup chicken broth
- 1/4 cup green olives, pitted
- 2 tablespoons fresh cilantro, chopped
- Salt and pepper to taste

Instructions:
1. Season the chicken thighs with salt and pepper on both sides.
2. Heat the olive oil in a tagine or a large, deep skillet over medium-high heat.
3. Add the chicken thighs to the tagine and cook until browned on both sides, about 5 minutes per side. Remove the chicken from the tagine and set aside.
4. In the same tagine, add the chopped onion and minced garlic. Cook until the onion is translucent and fragrant, about 5 minutes.

5. Add the ground cumin, coriander, paprika, turmeric, cinnamon, and cayenne pepper (if using) to the tagine. Stir well to coat the onions and garlic with the spices.
6. Return the chicken thighs to the tagine and add the preserved lemons, chicken broth, and green olives. Stir gently to combine.
7. Reduce the heat to low, cover the tagine with its lid, and simmer for 1 hour, or until the chicken is tender and cooked through.
8. Remove the lid and sprinkle the chopped cilantro over the chicken. Cook for an additional 5 minutes to allow the flavors to meld together.
9. Serve the Moroccan Chicken Tagine with Preserved Lemons hot, with couscous or crusty bread on the side.

Nutrition information per Serving: - Calories: 380
- Fat: 22g
- Carbohydrates: 10g
- Protein: 35g
- Fiber: 3g
- Sugar: 2g
- Sodium: 780mg

7. Lamb and Apricot Tagine

Lamb and Apricot Tagine is a delicious Moroccan dish that combines tender lamb with the sweetness of apricots and the aromatic flavors of various spices. This slow-cooked stew is perfect for a cozy dinner, as it fills your home with a tantalizing aroma and warms your soul with every bite.
Serving: 4 servings
Preparation time: 20 minutes
Ready time: 2 hours 30 minutes

Ingredients:
- 1.5 pounds (700g) lamb shoulder, cut into chunks
- 1 onion, finely chopped
- 3 cloves of garlic, minced
- 1 teaspoon ground cumin
- 1 teaspoon ground coriander
- 1 teaspoon ground cinnamon

- 1 teaspoon ground ginger
- 1/2 teaspoon ground turmeric
- 1/2 teaspoon paprika
- 1/4 teaspoon cayenne pepper (optional, for heat)
- 1 cup dried apricots
- 2 cups chicken or vegetable broth
- 2 tablespoons olive oil
- Salt and pepper, to taste
- Fresh cilantro or parsley, for garnish

Instructions:

1. In a large pot or tagine, heat the olive oil over medium heat. Add the lamb chunks and brown them on all sides. Remove the lamb from the pot and set aside.
2. In the same pot, add the chopped onion and minced garlic. Sauté until the onion becomes translucent and fragrant.
3. Add the ground cumin, coriander, cinnamon, ginger, turmeric, paprika, and cayenne pepper (if using) to the pot. Stir well to coat the onions and garlic with the spices.
4. Return the browned lamb to the pot and mix it with the onion and spice mixture. Season with salt and pepper to taste.
5. Pour in the chicken or vegetable broth, ensuring that the lamb is fully submerged. Bring the mixture to a boil, then reduce the heat to low and cover the pot. Let it simmer for about 2 hours, or until the lamb becomes tender and starts to fall apart.
6. Add the dried apricots to the pot and stir them into the stew. Cover the pot again and let it simmer for an additional 30 minutes, allowing the flavors to meld together.
7. Once the lamb is tender and the apricots have softened, remove the pot from the heat. Serve the Lamb and Apricot Tagine hot, garnished with fresh cilantro or parsley.

Nutrition information:

- Calories: 420
- Fat: 18g
- Carbohydrates: 32g
- Protein: 34g
- Fiber: 5g
- Sugar: 23g
- Sodium: 600mg

Note: Nutrition information may vary depending on the specific Ingredients and quantities used.

8. Vegetable and Chickpea Tagine

Vegetable and Chickpea Tagine is a delicious and nutritious Moroccan-inspired dish that is packed with flavor. This vegetarian recipe combines a variety of vegetables, aromatic spices, and protein-rich chickpeas to create a hearty and satisfying meal. The slow-cooking process allows the flavors to meld together, resulting in a dish that is both comforting and full of vibrant flavors.
Serving: 4 servings
Preparation time: 15 minutes
Ready time: 1 hour 30 minutes

Ingredients:
- 2 tablespoons olive oil
- 1 onion, diced
- 3 cloves garlic, minced
- 1 teaspoon ground cumin
- 1 teaspoon ground coriander
- 1 teaspoon ground turmeric
- 1 teaspoon paprika
- 1/2 teaspoon ground cinnamon
- 1/4 teaspoon cayenne pepper (optional, for heat)
- 1 red bell pepper, diced
- 1 yellow bell pepper, diced
- 2 carrots, peeled and sliced
- 1 zucchini, sliced
- 1 eggplant, diced
- 1 can (14 ounces) diced tomatoes
- 1 can (14 ounces) chickpeas, drained and rinsed
- 1 cup vegetable broth
- Salt and pepper to taste
- Fresh cilantro or parsley, chopped (for garnish)

Instructions:

1. Heat the olive oil in a large pot or tagine over medium heat. Add the diced onion and minced garlic, and sauté until the onion becomes translucent and fragrant.
2. Add the ground cumin, ground coriander, ground turmeric, paprika, ground cinnamon, and cayenne pepper (if using) to the pot. Stir well to coat the onions and garlic with the spices, and cook for an additional minute to toast the spices.
3. Add the diced red and yellow bell peppers, sliced carrots, sliced zucchini, and diced eggplant to the pot. Stir to combine the vegetables with the spices.
4. Pour in the diced tomatoes, drained and rinsed chickpeas, and vegetable broth. Season with salt and pepper to taste. Stir everything together, then cover the pot and reduce the heat to low.
5. Allow the tagine to simmer for 1 hour, or until the vegetables are tender and the flavors have melded together. Stir occasionally to prevent sticking.
6. Once the tagine is ready, taste and adjust the seasoning if needed. Serve hot, garnished with fresh cilantro or parsley.

Nutrition information per Serving: - Calories: 250
- Fat: 8g
- Carbohydrates: 38g
- Fiber: 10g
- Protein: 10g
- Sodium: 480mg

Note: Nutrition information may vary depending on the specific Ingredients and brands used.

9. Spicy Shrimp Tagine

Spicy Shrimp Tagine is a delicious and flavorful dish that combines succulent shrimp with a blend of aromatic spices and vegetables. This Moroccan-inspired recipe is perfect for those who enjoy a bit of heat and exotic flavors. The tagine cooking method ensures that all the Ingredients are cooked to perfection, resulting in a mouthwatering dish that will impress your family and friends.
Serving: 4 servings
Preparation time: 15 minutes

Ready time: 45 minutes

Ingredients:
- 1 pound of large shrimp, peeled and deveined
- 2 tablespoons of olive oil
- 1 onion, finely chopped
- 3 cloves of garlic, minced
- 1 red bell pepper, sliced
- 1 yellow bell pepper, sliced
- 1 teaspoon of ground cumin
- 1 teaspoon of ground coriander
- 1 teaspoon of paprika
- 1/2 teaspoon of cayenne pepper (adjust according to your spice preference)
- 1 can (14 ounces) of diced tomatoes
- 1/2 cup of chicken broth
- Salt and pepper to taste
- Fresh cilantro, chopped (for garnish)

Instructions:
1. Heat the olive oil in a tagine or a large skillet over medium heat.
2. Add the chopped onion and minced garlic to the tagine and sauté until they become translucent and fragrant.
3. Add the sliced bell peppers to the tagine and cook for another 3-4 minutes until they start to soften.
4. In a small bowl, combine the ground cumin, coriander, paprika, and cayenne pepper. Mix well.
5. Sprinkle the spice mixture over the vegetables in the tagine and stir to coat them evenly.
6. Add the diced tomatoes and chicken broth to the tagine, stirring well to combine all the Ingredients.
7. Bring the mixture to a simmer and let it cook for about 10 minutes, allowing the flavors to meld together.
8. Season the shrimp with salt and pepper, then add them to the tagine. Cook for an additional 5-7 minutes until the shrimp turn pink and are cooked through.
9. Remove the tagine from the heat and garnish with freshly chopped cilantro.
10. Serve the Spicy Shrimp Tagine hot with couscous or crusty bread.

Nutrition information per Serving: - Calories: 250
- Fat: 10g
- Carbohydrates: 12g
- Protein: 25g
- Fiber: 3g
- Sodium: 500mg

10. Moroccan Meatball Tagine

Moroccan Meatball Tagine is a flavorful and aromatic dish that combines tender meatballs with a rich tomato-based sauce. This traditional Moroccan recipe is packed with spices and herbs, creating a delicious and satisfying meal. Serve it with couscous or crusty bread for a complete and hearty dinner.
Serving: 4 servings
Preparation time: 20 minutes
Ready time: 1 hour 30 minutes

Ingredients:
- 500g ground beef or lamb
- 1 onion, finely chopped
- 3 cloves of garlic, minced
- 2 tablespoons fresh parsley, chopped
- 2 tablespoons fresh cilantro, chopped
- 1 teaspoon ground cumin
- 1 teaspoon ground coriander
- 1 teaspoon paprika
- 1/2 teaspoon ground cinnamon
- 1/2 teaspoon ground ginger
- 1/4 teaspoon cayenne pepper (optional, for heat)
- Salt and pepper to taste
- 2 tablespoons olive oil
- 1 can (400g) diced tomatoes
- 1 cup beef or vegetable broth
- 1 tablespoon tomato paste
- 1 tablespoon honey
- 1 preserved lemon, sliced (optional, for tanginess)
- Olives, for garnish

- Fresh cilantro, for garnish

Instructions:

1. In a large bowl, combine the ground meat, onion, garlic, parsley, cilantro, cumin, coriander, paprika, cinnamon, ginger, cayenne pepper (if using), salt, and pepper. Mix well until all the Ingredients are evenly incorporated.
2. Shape the mixture into small meatballs, about 1 inch in diameter.
3. Heat the olive oil in a tagine or a large, deep skillet over medium heat. Add the meatballs and cook until browned on all sides, about 5 minutes. Remove the meatballs from the tagine and set aside.
4. In the same tagine or skillet, add the diced tomatoes, broth, tomato paste, and honey. Stir well to combine.
5. Return the meatballs to the tagine and add the preserved lemon slices (if using). Cover and simmer over low heat for 1 hour, stirring occasionally.
6. Taste and adjust the seasoning if needed. If the sauce is too thick, add a little more broth or water.
7. Garnish with olives and fresh cilantro before serving.
8. Serve the Moroccan Meatball Tagine hot with couscous or crusty bread.

Nutrition information per Serving: - Calories: 350

- Fat: 20g
- Carbohydrates: 15g
- Protein: 25g
- Fiber: 3g
- Sugar: 7g
- Sodium: 600mg

11. Lemon and Olive Chicken Tagine

Lemon and Olive Chicken Tagine is a delicious and aromatic Moroccan dish that combines tender chicken with the tangy flavors of lemon and the briny taste of olives. This dish is slow-cooked in a traditional tagine pot, allowing all the flavors to meld together and create a mouthwatering meal. Serve it with couscous or crusty bread for a complete and satisfying dinner.

Serving: 4 servings
Preparation time: 15 minutes
Ready time: 1 hour 30 minutes

Ingredients:
- 4 chicken thighs, bone-in and skin-on
- 2 tablespoons olive oil
- 1 onion, thinly sliced
- 3 cloves of garlic, minced
- 1 teaspoon ground cumin
- 1 teaspoon ground coriander
- 1 teaspoon ground paprika
- 1 preserved lemon, flesh removed and rind thinly sliced
- 1 cup green olives, pitted
- 1 cup chicken broth
- 2 tablespoons fresh lemon juice
- Salt and pepper to taste
- Fresh cilantro, chopped (for garnish)

Instructions:
1. Heat the olive oil in a tagine pot or a large, heavy-bottomed skillet over medium heat.
2. Season the chicken thighs with salt and pepper, then add them to the pot, skin-side down. Cook until the skin is golden brown and crispy, about 5 minutes. Flip the chicken and cook for an additional 3 minutes. Remove the chicken from the pot and set aside.
3. In the same pot, add the sliced onion and minced garlic. Sauté until the onion becomes translucent and fragrant, about 5 minutes.
4. Add the ground cumin, coriander, and paprika to the pot. Stir well to coat the onions and garlic with the spices.
5. Return the chicken thighs to the pot, along with the preserved lemon slices and green olives. Pour in the chicken broth and lemon juice. Stir gently to combine all the Ingredients.
6. Cover the pot and reduce the heat to low. Allow the tagine to simmer for 1 hour, or until the chicken is tender and cooked through.
7. Taste the sauce and adjust the seasoning with salt and pepper if needed.
8. Serve the Lemon and Olive Chicken Tagine hot, garnished with fresh cilantro. It pairs well with couscous or crusty bread.

Nutrition information (per serving):
- Calories: 380
- Fat: 24g
- Carbohydrates: 10g
- Protein: 30g
- Fiber: 3g

12. Vegetable Tagine with Harissa Sauce

Vegetable Tagine with Harissa Sauce is a flavorful and aromatic Moroccan dish that combines a variety of vegetables with a spicy and tangy harissa sauce. This vegetarian dish is not only delicious but also packed with nutrients, making it a perfect choice for a healthy and satisfying meal.
Serving: 4 servings
Preparation time: 15 minutes
Ready time: 1 hour

Ingredients:
- 2 tablespoons olive oil
- 1 onion, diced
- 3 cloves of garlic, minced
- 1 teaspoon ground cumin
- 1 teaspoon ground coriander
- 1 teaspoon ground turmeric
- 1 teaspoon paprika
- 1 teaspoon cinnamon
- 1 teaspoon salt
- 1/2 teaspoon black pepper
- 1/4 teaspoon cayenne pepper (optional, for extra heat)
- 2 carrots, peeled and sliced
- 2 zucchinis, sliced
- 1 red bell pepper, sliced
- 1 yellow bell pepper, sliced
- 1 eggplant, diced
- 1 can (14 oz) diced tomatoes
- 1 cup vegetable broth
- 2 tablespoons harissa paste

- 1 tablespoon honey (optional, for a touch of sweetness)
- Fresh cilantro or parsley, chopped (for garnish)

Instructions:
1. Heat the olive oil in a large pot or tagine over medium heat. Add the diced onion and minced garlic, and sauté until they become translucent and fragrant.
2. In a small bowl, mix together the ground cumin, coriander, turmeric, paprika, cinnamon, salt, black pepper, and cayenne pepper (if using). Add this spice mixture to the pot and stir well to coat the onions and garlic.
3. Add the sliced carrots, zucchinis, red and yellow bell peppers, and diced eggplant to the pot. Stir everything together to combine the vegetables with the spices.
4. Pour in the diced tomatoes and vegetable broth. Stir well and bring the mixture to a simmer. Cover the pot and let it cook for about 45 minutes to 1 hour, or until the vegetables are tender.
5. In a small bowl, mix together the harissa paste and honey (if using). Add this mixture to the pot and stir well to incorporate the flavors. Let the tagine simmer for an additional 5 minutes.
6. Serve the Vegetable Tagine with Harissa Sauce hot, garnished with fresh cilantro or parsley. It can be enjoyed on its own or served with couscous or crusty bread.

Nutrition information per Serving: - Calories: 180
- Fat: 7g
- Carbohydrates: 28g
- Fiber: 8g
- Protein: 4g
- Sodium: 800mg

13. Beef and Vegetable Tagine

Beef and Vegetable Tagine is a flavorful and aromatic Moroccan dish that combines tender beef, a medley of vegetables, and a blend of warm spices. This slow-cooked stew is perfect for a cozy dinner, as it fills your home with delightful scents and offers a comforting and hearty meal. Serve it with couscous or crusty bread for a complete and satisfying dining experience.

Serving: 4 servings
Preparation time: 20 minutes
Ready time: 2 hours 30 minutes

Ingredients:
- 1.5 pounds beef stew meat, cut into chunks
- 2 tablespoons olive oil
- 1 onion, diced
- 3 cloves garlic, minced
- 2 carrots, peeled and sliced
- 2 bell peppers, diced
- 1 zucchini, sliced
- 1 cup diced tomatoes
- 1 cup beef broth
- 1 tablespoon tomato paste
- 1 teaspoon ground cumin
- 1 teaspoon ground coriander
- 1 teaspoon ground paprika
- 1 teaspoon ground turmeric
- 1/2 teaspoon ground cinnamon
- Salt and pepper to taste
- Fresh cilantro or parsley, chopped (for garnish)

Instructions:
1. Heat the olive oil in a large, heavy-bottomed pot or tagine over medium heat. Add the beef chunks and brown them on all sides. Remove the beef from the pot and set it aside.
2. In the same pot, add the diced onion and minced garlic. Sauté until the onion becomes translucent and fragrant.
3. Add the carrots, bell peppers, and zucchini to the pot. Cook for about 5 minutes, until the vegetables start to soften.
4. Return the beef to the pot and add the diced tomatoes, beef broth, and tomato paste. Stir well to combine.
5. Sprinkle in the ground cumin, coriander, paprika, turmeric, cinnamon, salt, and pepper. Stir again to evenly distribute the spices.
6. Cover the pot and reduce the heat to low. Let the tagine simmer for about 2 hours, or until the beef is tender and the flavors have melded together.
7. Once the tagine is ready, taste and adjust the seasoning if needed. Garnish with fresh cilantro or parsley before serving.

8. Serve the Beef and Vegetable Tagine hot with couscous or crusty bread.

Nutrition information per Serving: - Calories: 380
- Fat: 18g
- Carbohydrates: 20g
- Protein: 34g
- Fiber: 5g
- Sugar: 9g
- Sodium: 600mg

14. Fish Tagine with Tomatoes and Peppers

Fish Tagine with Tomatoes and Peppers is a delicious and flavorful dish that originates from North Africa. This dish is known for its aromatic spices and tender fish, cooked in a traditional tagine pot. The combination of tomatoes, peppers, and spices creates a rich and savory sauce that perfectly complements the delicate fish. This recipe is easy to make and is sure to impress your family and friends.
Serving: 4 servings
Preparation time: 15 minutes
Ready time: 45 minutes

Ingredients:
- 4 fish fillets (such as cod, halibut, or sea bass)
- 2 tablespoons olive oil
- 1 onion, thinly sliced
- 2 garlic cloves, minced
- 1 red bell pepper, thinly sliced
- 1 yellow bell pepper, thinly sliced
- 1 can (400g) diced tomatoes
- 1 teaspoon ground cumin
- 1 teaspoon ground paprika
- 1 teaspoon ground turmeric
- 1 teaspoon ground ginger
- Salt and pepper to taste
- Fresh cilantro or parsley, chopped (for garnish)

Instructions:
1. Heat the olive oil in a tagine pot or a large skillet over medium heat.
2. Add the sliced onion and minced garlic to the pot and sauté until they become translucent and fragrant.
3. Add the sliced bell peppers to the pot and cook for another 3-4 minutes until they start to soften.
4. Stir in the diced tomatoes, cumin, paprika, turmeric, ginger, salt, and pepper. Allow the mixture to simmer for about 10 minutes, stirring occasionally.
5. Gently place the fish fillets on top of the tomato and pepper mixture in the pot. Cover the pot and let it simmer for 15-20 minutes, or until the fish is cooked through and flakes easily with a fork.
6. Once the fish is cooked, remove the pot from the heat and garnish with fresh cilantro or parsley.
7. Serve the Fish Tagine with Tomatoes and Peppers hot, accompanied by couscous or crusty bread.

Nutrition information:
- Calories: 250 per Serving: - Fat: 10g
- Carbohydrates: 10g
- Protein: 30g
- Fiber: 3g
- Sodium: 400mg

15. Moroccan Chicken Tagine with Olives and Tomatoes

Moroccan Chicken Tagine with Olives and Tomatoes is a flavorful and aromatic dish that combines tender chicken, briny olives, and juicy tomatoes. This traditional Moroccan recipe is cooked in a tagine, a clay pot with a conical lid, which helps to infuse the dish with rich flavors. The combination of spices and Ingredients creates a deliciously satisfying meal that is perfect for any occasion.
Serving: 4 servings
Preparation time: 15 minutes
Ready time: 1 hour 30 minutes

Ingredients:

- 4 chicken thighs, bone-in and skin-on
- 2 tablespoons olive oil
- 1 onion, finely chopped
- 3 cloves of garlic, minced
- 1 teaspoon ground cumin
- 1 teaspoon ground coriander
- 1 teaspoon ground paprika
- 1 teaspoon ground turmeric
- 1 teaspoon ground cinnamon
- 1 teaspoon salt
- 1/2 teaspoon black pepper
- 1 cup chicken broth
- 1 cup canned diced tomatoes
- 1/2 cup green olives, pitted
- 1/4 cup fresh cilantro, chopped
- 1/4 cup fresh parsley, chopped
- Lemon wedges, for Serving:

Instructions:

1. Heat the olive oil in a tagine or a large, deep skillet over medium heat. Add the chicken thighs, skin side down, and cook until browned, about 5 minutes. Flip the chicken and brown the other side for an additional 5 minutes. Remove the chicken from the tagine and set aside.
2. In the same tagine, add the chopped onion and minced garlic. Sauté until the onion becomes translucent, about 5 minutes.
3. Add the ground cumin, coriander, paprika, turmeric, cinnamon, salt, and black pepper to the tagine. Stir well to coat the onions and garlic with the spices.
4. Pour in the chicken broth and canned diced tomatoes. Stir to combine.
5. Return the chicken thighs to the tagine, nestling them into the sauce. Cover with the lid and simmer over low heat for 1 hour, or until the chicken is cooked through and tender.
6. Add the green olives to the tagine and simmer for an additional 10 minutes to allow the flavors to meld together.
7. Sprinkle the chopped cilantro and parsley over the top of the tagine before serving.
8. Serve the Moroccan Chicken Tagine with Olives and Tomatoes hot, accompanied by lemon wedges for squeezing over the dish.

Nutrition information per Serving: - Calories: 380

- Fat: 24g
- Carbohydrates: 10g
- Protein: 30g
- Fiber: 3g

16. Lamb and Date Tagine

Lamb and Date Tagine is a delicious Moroccan dish that combines tender lamb with sweet dates and aromatic spices. This slow-cooked stew is full of flavor and perfect for a cozy dinner on a chilly evening. The combination of savory and sweet flavors makes this dish truly unique and satisfying.
Serving: 4 servings
Preparation time: 20 minutes
Ready time: 2 hours 30 minutes

Ingredients:
- 1.5 pounds lamb shoulder, cut into chunks
- 1 onion, finely chopped
- 3 cloves of garlic, minced
- 1 teaspoon ground cumin
- 1 teaspoon ground coriander
- 1 teaspoon ground cinnamon
- 1 teaspoon ground ginger
- 1 teaspoon paprika
- 1/2 teaspoon turmeric
- 1/2 teaspoon cayenne pepper (optional, for heat)
- 1 cup pitted dates
- 1 cup chicken or vegetable broth
- 2 tablespoons olive oil
- Salt and pepper to taste
- Fresh cilantro, chopped (for garnish)

Instructions:
1. In a large tagine or a heavy-bottomed pot, heat the olive oil over medium heat. Add the lamb chunks and brown them on all sides. Remove the lamb from the pot and set aside.

2. In the same pot, add the chopped onion and minced garlic. Sauté until the onion becomes translucent and fragrant.
3. Add the ground cumin, coriander, cinnamon, ginger, paprika, turmeric, and cayenne pepper (if using) to the pot. Stir well to coat the onions and garlic with the spices.
4. Return the browned lamb to the pot and mix it with the onion and spice mixture. Season with salt and pepper to taste.
5. Pour in the chicken or vegetable broth and bring the mixture to a simmer. Cover the pot and let it cook on low heat for about 2 hours, or until the lamb becomes tender and starts to fall apart.
6. Add the pitted dates to the pot and stir them into the stew. Cover the pot again and let it cook for an additional 30 minutes, allowing the flavors to meld together.
7. Once the lamb is tender and the dates have softened, remove the pot from the heat. Serve the Lamb and Date Tagine hot, garnished with fresh chopped cilantro.

Nutrition information:
- Calories: 420
- Fat: 18g
- Carbohydrates: 30g
- Protein: 35g
- Fiber: 4g
- Sodium: 450mg

Note: Nutrition information may vary depending on the specific Ingredients and brands used.

17. Chickpea and Spinach Tagine

Chickpea and Spinach Tagine is a flavorful and nutritious dish that combines the earthy flavors of chickpeas and the vibrant freshness of spinach. This Moroccan-inspired recipe is not only delicious but also easy to prepare, making it a perfect choice for a quick and healthy weeknight meal.
Serving: 4 servings
Preparation time: 10 minutes
Ready time: 30 minutes

Ingredients:
- 2 tablespoons olive oil
- 1 onion, finely chopped
- 3 cloves of garlic, minced
- 1 teaspoon ground cumin
- 1 teaspoon ground coriander
- 1 teaspoon ground paprika
- 1/2 teaspoon ground turmeric
- 1/4 teaspoon cayenne pepper (optional, for heat)
- 1 can (14 ounces) chickpeas, drained and rinsed
- 1 can (14 ounces) diced tomatoes
- 1 cup vegetable broth
- 4 cups fresh spinach leaves
- Salt and pepper to taste
- Fresh cilantro, chopped (for garnish)

Instructions:
1. Heat the olive oil in a large pot or tagine over medium heat. Add the chopped onion and minced garlic, and sauté until the onion becomes translucent and fragrant, about 5 minutes.
2. Add the ground cumin, coriander, paprika, turmeric, and cayenne pepper (if using) to the pot. Stir well to coat the onions and garlic with the spices, and cook for an additional 1-2 minutes to toast the spices.
3. Add the drained chickpeas, diced tomatoes, and vegetable broth to the pot. Stir everything together, then bring the mixture to a simmer. Reduce the heat to low, cover the pot, and let it cook for 15 minutes to allow the flavors to meld together.
4. After 15 minutes, remove the lid and add the fresh spinach leaves to the pot. Stir well to combine, and cook for an additional 5 minutes until the spinach wilts and becomes tender. Season with salt and pepper to taste.
5. Serve the Chickpea and Spinach Tagine hot, garnished with fresh chopped cilantro. It can be enjoyed on its own as a vegetarian main dish or served with couscous or crusty bread for a heartier meal.

Nutrition information per Serving: - Calories: 220
- Fat: 8g
- Carbohydrates: 30g
- Fiber: 8g
- Protein: 9g

- Sodium: 480mg

18. Spicy Harissa Chicken Tagine

Spicy Harissa Chicken Tagine is a flavorful and aromatic Moroccan dish that combines tender chicken with a spicy and tangy harissa sauce. This dish is perfect for those who enjoy a bit of heat and love the exotic flavors of North African cuisine. With a combination of spices and herbs, this tagine is sure to impress your taste buds and transport you to the vibrant streets of Morocco.
Serving: 4 servings
Preparation time: 15 minutes
Ready time: 1 hour 30 minutes

Ingredients:
- 4 chicken thighs, bone-in and skin-on
- 2 tablespoons olive oil
- 1 onion, finely chopped
- 3 cloves of garlic, minced
- 2 tablespoons harissa paste
- 1 teaspoon ground cumin
- 1 teaspoon ground coriander
- 1 teaspoon ground paprika
- 1 teaspoon ground turmeric
- 1 teaspoon ground cinnamon
- 1 cup chicken broth
- 1 cup canned diced tomatoes
- 1 tablespoon honey
- Salt and pepper to taste
- Fresh cilantro, chopped (for garnish)

Instructions:
1. In a large tagine or a deep, heavy-bottomed skillet, heat the olive oil over medium heat. Add the chicken thighs, skin-side down, and cook until browned, about 5 minutes. Flip the chicken and brown the other side for an additional 5 minutes. Remove the chicken from the tagine and set aside.

2. In the same tagine, add the chopped onion and minced garlic. Sauté until the onion becomes translucent and fragrant, about 5 minutes.
3. Add the harissa paste, ground cumin, ground coriander, ground paprika, ground turmeric, and ground cinnamon to the tagine. Stir well to coat the onions and garlic with the spices.
4. Pour in the chicken broth and canned diced tomatoes. Stir in the honey and season with salt and pepper to taste. Bring the mixture to a simmer.
5. Return the chicken thighs to the tagine, nestling them into the sauce. Cover the tagine and let it simmer over low heat for 1 hour, or until the chicken is cooked through and tender.
6. Once the chicken is cooked, remove the tagine from the heat. Garnish with fresh cilantro.
7. Serve the Spicy Harissa Chicken Tagine hot with couscous or crusty bread.

Nutrition information:
- Calories: 350
- Fat: 20g
- Carbohydrates: 10g
- Protein: 30g
- Fiber: 2g
- Sodium: 600mg

Note: Nutrition information may vary depending on the specific Ingredients and brands used.

19. Vegetable Tagine with Ras el Hanout

Vegetable Tagine with Ras el Hanout is a delicious and aromatic Moroccan dish that is packed with flavors. This vegetarian tagine is made with a variety of vegetables cooked in a flavorful blend of spices known as Ras el Hanout. It is a perfect dish to warm you up on a cold day and is sure to impress your family and friends with its vibrant colors and exotic taste.
Serving: 4 servings
Preparation time: 15 minutes
Ready time: 1 hour

Ingredients:
- 2 tablespoons olive oil
- 1 onion, diced
- 3 cloves of garlic, minced
- 1 teaspoon ground cumin
- 1 teaspoon ground coriander
- 1 teaspoon ground ginger
- 1 teaspoon ground cinnamon
- 1 teaspoon paprika
- 1 teaspoon turmeric
- 1 teaspoon Ras el Hanout spice blend
- 1 can (400g) diced tomatoes
- 2 cups vegetable broth
- 1 sweet potato, peeled and diced
- 2 carrots, peeled and sliced
- 1 zucchini, sliced
- 1 red bell pepper, sliced
- 1 cup cauliflower florets
- 1 cup chickpeas, cooked or canned
- Salt and pepper to taste
- Fresh cilantro or parsley, chopped (for garnish)

Instructions:
1. Heat the olive oil in a large pot or tagine over medium heat. Add the diced onion and minced garlic, and sauté until the onion becomes translucent.
2. Add the ground cumin, coriander, ginger, cinnamon, paprika, turmeric, and Ras el Hanout spice blend to the pot. Stir well to coat the onions and garlic with the spices.
3. Pour in the diced tomatoes and vegetable broth, and bring the mixture to a simmer.
4. Add the sweet potato, carrots, zucchini, red bell pepper, cauliflower florets, and chickpeas to the pot. Stir to combine all the Ingredients.
5. Season with salt and pepper to taste. Cover the pot and let the tagine simmer for about 45 minutes to 1 hour, or until the vegetables are tender.
6. Once the vegetables are cooked, remove the pot from the heat. Serve the Vegetable Tagine with Ras el Hanout hot, garnished with fresh cilantro or parsley.

Nutrition information per Serving: - Calories: 250
- Fat: 8g
- Carbohydrates: 40g
- Fiber: 10g
- Protein: 8g
- Sodium: 600mg

Note: Nutrition information may vary depending on the specific Ingredients and brands used.

20. Beef and Prune Tagine with Almonds

Beef and Prune Tagine with Almonds is a delicious and aromatic Moroccan dish that combines tender beef, sweet prunes, and crunchy almonds. This hearty and flavorful tagine is perfect for a cozy dinner or special occasions. The slow cooking process allows the flavors to meld together, resulting in a dish that is rich and satisfying. Serve it with couscous or crusty bread for a complete meal.
Serving: 4 servings
Preparation time: 15 minutes
Ready time: 2 hours 30 minutes

Ingredients:
- 1.5 pounds beef stew meat, cut into chunks
- 1 onion, finely chopped
- 3 cloves garlic, minced
- 1 teaspoon ground cumin
- 1 teaspoon ground coriander
- 1 teaspoon ground cinnamon
- 1 teaspoon paprika
- 1/2 teaspoon ground ginger
- 1/4 teaspoon cayenne pepper (optional, for heat)
- 1 cup pitted prunes
- 1/2 cup whole almonds
- 2 cups beef broth
- 2 tablespoons olive oil
- Salt and pepper to taste
- Fresh cilantro or parsley, for garnish

Instructions:

1. In a large tagine or heavy-bottomed pot, heat the olive oil over medium heat. Add the chopped onion and minced garlic, and sauté until they become translucent and fragrant.
2. Add the beef stew meat to the pot and brown it on all sides. This will help seal in the juices and add flavor to the dish.
3. Once the beef is browned, add the ground cumin, coriander, cinnamon, paprika, ginger, and cayenne pepper (if using). Stir well to coat the meat with the spices.
4. Pour in the beef broth and bring the mixture to a simmer. Cover the pot and let it cook on low heat for about 2 hours, or until the beef becomes tender and easily falls apart.
5. After 2 hours, add the pitted prunes and whole almonds to the pot. Stir gently to combine all the Ingredients.
6. Cover the pot again and let it simmer for an additional 30 minutes, or until the prunes plump up and the flavors meld together.
7. Season with salt and pepper to taste. If the sauce is too thin, you can simmer it uncovered for a few more minutes to thicken it slightly.
8. Serve the Beef and Prune Tagine with Almonds hot, garnished with fresh cilantro or parsley. It pairs well with couscous or crusty bread.

Nutrition information:

- Calories: 420
- Fat: 18g
- Carbohydrates: 30g
- Protein: 35g
- Fiber: 5g
- Sugar: 15g
- Sodium: 600mg

21. Fish Tagine with Preserved Lemons and Olives

Fish Tagine with Preserved Lemons and Olives is a traditional Moroccan dish that combines the delicate flavors of fish with the tanginess of preserved lemons and the brininess of olives. This aromatic and flavorful dish is cooked in a tagine, a traditional clay pot, which helps to infuse the Ingredients with rich flavors. It is a perfect dish to impress your guests or to enjoy as a special meal at home.

Serving: 4 servings
Preparation time: 20 minutes
Ready time: 1 hour 30 minutes

Ingredients:
- 4 fish fillets (such as cod, halibut, or sea bass)
- 2 preserved lemons, rinsed and thinly sliced
- 1 cup green olives, pitted
- 1 onion, finely chopped
- 3 cloves of garlic, minced
- 2 tablespoons olive oil
- 1 teaspoon ground cumin
- 1 teaspoon ground coriander
- 1 teaspoon paprika
- 1 teaspoon turmeric
- 1/2 teaspoon ground ginger
- 1/2 teaspoon ground cinnamon
- 1/4 teaspoon cayenne pepper (optional, for heat)
- 1 cup vegetable or fish broth
- Salt and pepper to taste
- Fresh cilantro or parsley, chopped (for garnish)

Instructions:
1. Preheat your oven to 350°F (175°C).
2. In a large tagine or oven-safe pot, heat the olive oil over medium heat. Add the chopped onion and minced garlic, and sauté until they become translucent and fragrant.
3. In a small bowl, mix together the ground cumin, coriander, paprika, turmeric, ginger, cinnamon, cayenne pepper (if using), salt, and pepper. Sprinkle this spice mixture over the sautéed onions and garlic, and stir well to coat.
4. Place the fish fillets on top of the spiced onion mixture in the tagine. Arrange the preserved lemon slices and green olives around the fish.
5. Pour the vegetable or fish broth into the tagine, ensuring that it covers the fish fillets partially. If needed, add more broth or water.
6. Cover the tagine with its lid or use aluminum foil to tightly cover the pot. Transfer the tagine to the preheated oven and bake for approximately 1 hour, or until the fish is cooked through and flakes easily with a fork.

7. Once cooked, remove the tagine from the oven and let it rest for a few minutes. Garnish with freshly chopped cilantro or parsley.
8. Serve the Fish Tagine with Preserved Lemons and Olives hot, accompanied by couscous or crusty bread.

Nutrition information per Serving: - Calories: 280
- Fat: 12g
- Carbohydrates: 10g
- Protein: 32g
- Fiber: 3g
- Sodium: 900mg

Note: Nutrition information may vary depending on the type of fish used and the specific brand of preserved lemons and olives.

22. Moroccan Chicken Tagine with Caramelized Onions

Moroccan Chicken Tagine with Caramelized Onions is a flavorful and aromatic dish that combines tender chicken with sweet caramelized onions and a blend of Moroccan spices. This traditional Moroccan dish is slow-cooked in a tagine, a clay pot with a conical lid, which helps to infuse the flavors and create a deliciously tender chicken. Serve this dish with couscous or crusty bread for a complete and satisfying meal.
Serving: 4 servings
Preparation time: 15 minutes
Ready time: 1 hour 30 minutes

Ingredients:
- 4 chicken thighs, bone-in and skin-on
- 2 large onions, thinly sliced
- 3 cloves of garlic, minced
- 2 teaspoons ground cumin
- 2 teaspoons ground coriander
- 1 teaspoon ground turmeric
- 1 teaspoon ground cinnamon
- 1 teaspoon paprika
- 1/2 teaspoon ground ginger
- 1/4 teaspoon cayenne pepper (optional, for heat)

- 1 cup chicken broth
- 1/4 cup olive oil
- 2 tablespoons honey
- Salt and pepper to taste
- Fresh cilantro, chopped (for garnish)

Instructions:
1. In a large bowl, combine the ground cumin, ground coriander, ground turmeric, ground cinnamon, paprika, ground ginger, cayenne pepper (if using), salt, and pepper. Mix well to create a spice rub.
2. Rub the spice mixture all over the chicken thighs, ensuring they are evenly coated. Set aside to marinate for at least 30 minutes.
3. In a tagine or a large, deep skillet, heat the olive oil over medium heat. Add the sliced onions and cook until they are caramelized and golden brown, stirring occasionally. This process may take about 20-25 minutes.
4. Once the onions are caramelized, add the minced garlic to the tagine and cook for an additional 1-2 minutes until fragrant.
5. Push the onions and garlic to the sides of the tagine, creating a well in the center. Place the marinated chicken thighs in the center of the tagine and sear them on both sides until browned, about 3-4 minutes per side.
6. Pour the chicken broth into the tagine, ensuring it covers the chicken thighs. Drizzle the honey over the chicken.
7. Reduce the heat to low, cover the tagine with its lid, and simmer for 1 hour, or until the chicken is cooked through and tender.
8. Once the chicken is cooked, remove it from the tagine and set aside. Increase the heat to medium-high and cook the sauce uncovered for an additional 10-15 minutes, or until it thickens slightly.
9. Serve the chicken thighs with the caramelized onions and sauce spooned over the top. Garnish with fresh cilantro.
10. Enjoy your Moroccan Chicken Tagine with Caramelized Onions!

Nutrition information:
- Calories: 380
- Fat: 22g
- Carbohydrates: 18g
- Protein: 28g
- Fiber: 3g
- Sugar: 11g
- Sodium: 450mg

23. Lamb and Chickpea Tagine

Lamb and Chickpea Tagine is a flavorful and aromatic Moroccan dish that combines tender lamb, hearty chickpeas, and a blend of spices. This slow-cooked stew is perfect for a cozy dinner on a chilly evening. The combination of tender meat, creamy chickpeas, and fragrant spices will transport you to the vibrant streets of Morocco.
Serving: 4 servings
Preparation time: 20 minutes
Ready time: 2 hours 30 minutes

Ingredients:
- 1.5 pounds lamb shoulder, cut into chunks
- 1 onion, finely chopped
- 3 cloves of garlic, minced
- 1 teaspoon ground cumin
- 1 teaspoon ground coriander
- 1 teaspoon ground turmeric
- 1 teaspoon ground cinnamon
- 1 teaspoon paprika
- 1/2 teaspoon ground ginger
- 1/4 teaspoon cayenne pepper (optional, for heat)
- 1 can (14 ounces) diced tomatoes
- 1 can (14 ounces) chickpeas, drained and rinsed
- 1 cup chicken or vegetable broth
- 1 tablespoon honey
- 1 tablespoon olive oil
- Salt and pepper to taste
- Fresh cilantro, chopped (for garnish)

Instructions:
1. In a large pot or tagine, heat the olive oil over medium heat. Add the lamb chunks and brown them on all sides. Remove the lamb from the pot and set aside.
2. In the same pot, add the chopped onion and minced garlic. Sauté until the onion becomes translucent and fragrant.

3. Add the ground cumin, coriander, turmeric, cinnamon, paprika, ginger, and cayenne pepper (if using) to the pot. Stir well to coat the onions and garlic with the spices.
4. Return the browned lamb to the pot and mix it with the onion and spice mixture.
5. Pour in the diced tomatoes, chickpeas, and chicken or vegetable broth. Stir well to combine all the Ingredients.
6. Bring the mixture to a boil, then reduce the heat to low. Cover the pot and let it simmer for about 2 hours, or until the lamb is tender and the flavors have melded together.
7. Stir in the honey and season with salt and pepper to taste.
8. Serve the Lamb and Chickpea Tagine hot, garnished with fresh cilantro. It pairs well with couscous or crusty bread.

Nutrition information:
- Calories: 420
- Fat: 18g
- Carbohydrates: 28g
- Protein: 36g
- Fiber: 7g
- Sodium: 680mg

24. Vegetable Tagine with Moroccan Spices

Vegetable Tagine with Moroccan Spices is a flavorful and aromatic dish that combines a variety of vegetables with traditional Moroccan spices. This vegetarian dish is not only delicious but also packed with nutrients, making it a perfect choice for a healthy and satisfying meal.
Serving: 4 servings
Preparation time: 15 minutes
Ready time: 1 hour

Ingredients:
- 2 tablespoons olive oil
- 1 onion, diced
- 3 cloves of garlic, minced
- 1 teaspoon ground cumin
- 1 teaspoon ground coriander

- 1 teaspoon ground turmeric
- 1 teaspoon ground paprika
- 1/2 teaspoon ground cinnamon
- 1/4 teaspoon cayenne pepper (optional, for heat)
- 1 eggplant, cut into cubes
- 2 zucchinis, sliced
- 2 carrots, sliced
- 1 red bell pepper, sliced
- 1 can (14 oz) diced tomatoes
- 1 cup vegetable broth
- 1 cup chickpeas, cooked or canned
- Salt and pepper to taste
- Fresh cilantro or parsley, chopped (for garnish)

Instructions:
1. Heat the olive oil in a large pot or tagine over medium heat. Add the diced onion and minced garlic, and sauté until they become translucent and fragrant.
2. Add the ground cumin, coriander, turmeric, paprika, cinnamon, and cayenne pepper (if using) to the pot. Stir well to coat the onions and garlic with the spices, and cook for another minute to release their flavors.
3. Add the cubed eggplant, sliced zucchinis, carrots, and red bell pepper to the pot. Stir to combine the vegetables with the spices.
4. Pour in the diced tomatoes and vegetable broth. Bring the mixture to a simmer, then reduce the heat to low. Cover the pot and let it cook for about 45 minutes, or until the vegetables are tender.
5. Stir in the cooked or canned chickpeas, and season with salt and pepper to taste. Cook for an additional 5 minutes to heat the chickpeas through.
6. Remove the pot from the heat and let it sit for a few minutes before serving. Garnish with freshly chopped cilantro or parsley.

Nutrition information per Serving: - Calories: 220
- Fat: 8g
- Carbohydrates: 32g
- Fiber: 10g
- Protein: 8g
- Sodium: 480mg

Note: Nutrition information may vary depending on the specific Ingredients and brands used.

25. Spicy Harissa Shrimp Tagine

Spicy Harissa Shrimp Tagine is a delicious and flavorful dish that combines succulent shrimp with a spicy and aromatic harissa sauce. This North African-inspired recipe is perfect for those who enjoy a bit of heat in their meals. The combination of spices and herbs creates a tantalizing flavor that will leave you craving for more. Serve this dish with couscous or crusty bread for a complete and satisfying meal.
Serving: 4 servings
Preparation time: 15 minutes
Ready time: 30 minutes

Ingredients:
- 1 pound of large shrimp, peeled and deveined
- 2 tablespoons of olive oil
- 1 onion, finely chopped
- 3 cloves of garlic, minced
- 2 tablespoons of harissa paste
- 1 teaspoon of ground cumin
- 1 teaspoon of ground coriander
- 1 teaspoon of paprika
- 1 teaspoon of salt
- 1/2 teaspoon of black pepper
- 1 can (14 ounces) of diced tomatoes
- 1 cup of chicken broth
- 1 tablespoon of lemon juice
- Fresh cilantro, chopped (for garnish)

Instructions:
1. In a large skillet or tagine, heat the olive oil over medium heat. Add the chopped onion and minced garlic, and sauté until they become translucent and fragrant.
2. Add the harissa paste, ground cumin, ground coriander, paprika, salt, and black pepper to the skillet. Stir well to combine the spices with the onion and garlic mixture.

3. Add the diced tomatoes and chicken broth to the skillet. Stir everything together and let it simmer for about 10 minutes, allowing the flavors to meld together.
4. Add the peeled and deveined shrimp to the skillet. Cook for about 5-7 minutes, or until the shrimp turn pink and are cooked through.
5. Stir in the lemon juice and give it a final mix.
6. Serve the Spicy Harissa Shrimp Tagine hot, garnished with fresh chopped cilantro. It pairs well with couscous or crusty bread.

Nutrition information:
- Calories: 250
- Fat: 10g
- Carbohydrates: 10g
- Protein: 30g
- Fiber: 2g
- Sodium: 800mg

Note: Nutrition information may vary depending on the specific Ingredients and brands used.

26. Moroccan Meatball Tagine with Eggplant

Moroccan Meatball Tagine with Eggplant is a flavorful and aromatic dish that combines tender meatballs with the rich flavors of eggplant and Moroccan spices. This traditional Moroccan dish is perfect for a hearty and satisfying meal that will transport you to the vibrant streets of Morocco.
Serving: 4 servings
Preparation time: 20 minutes
Ready time: 1 hour 30 minutes

Ingredients:
- 1 lb ground beef
- 1 small onion, finely chopped
- 2 cloves of garlic, minced
- 1 teaspoon ground cumin
- 1 teaspoon ground coriander
- 1 teaspoon paprika
- 1/2 teaspoon ground cinnamon

- 1/2 teaspoon ground ginger
- 1/4 teaspoon cayenne pepper (optional, for heat)
- Salt and pepper to taste
- 1 egg, beaten
- 1/4 cup breadcrumbs
- 2 tablespoons olive oil
- 1 large eggplant, cut into 1-inch cubes
- 1 can (14 oz) diced tomatoes
- 1 cup chicken or vegetable broth
- Fresh cilantro, chopped (for garnish)

Instructions:

1. In a large bowl, combine the ground beef, onion, garlic, cumin, coriander, paprika, cinnamon, ginger, cayenne pepper (if using), salt, and pepper. Mix well until all the Ingredients are evenly incorporated.
2. Add the beaten egg and breadcrumbs to the meat mixture. Mix again until everything is well combined.
3. Shape the meat mixture into small meatballs, about 1 inch in diameter.
4. Heat the olive oil in a large tagine or a deep skillet over medium heat. Add the meatballs and cook until browned on all sides, about 5 minutes. Remove the meatballs from the tagine and set aside.
5. In the same tagine, add the cubed eggplant and cook for 5 minutes, stirring occasionally, until slightly softened.
6. Add the diced tomatoes and chicken or vegetable broth to the tagine. Stir well to combine.
7. Return the meatballs to the tagine, nestling them among the eggplant and tomato mixture.
8. Cover the tagine and simmer over low heat for 1 hour, or until the meatballs are cooked through and the flavors have melded together.
9. Serve the Moroccan Meatball Tagine with Eggplant hot, garnished with fresh cilantro. It pairs well with couscous or crusty bread.

Nutrition information per Serving: - Calories: 380
- Fat: 22g
- Carbohydrates: 18g
- Protein: 28g
- Fiber: 6g

27. Chicken and Vegetable Tagine with Saffron

Chicken and Vegetable Tagine with Saffron is a flavorful and aromatic Moroccan dish that combines tender chicken, vibrant vegetables, and fragrant saffron. This dish is perfect for those who enjoy a hearty and healthy meal with a touch of exotic flavors. The slow cooking process allows the flavors to meld together, resulting in a delicious and satisfying meal.

Serving: 4 servings

Preparation time: 15 minutes

Ready time: 1 hour 30 minutes

Ingredients:

- 4 chicken thighs, bone-in and skin-on
- 2 tablespoons olive oil
- 1 onion, thinly sliced
- 3 cloves of garlic, minced
- 1 teaspoon ground cumin
- 1 teaspoon ground coriander
- 1 teaspoon ground paprika
- 1/2 teaspoon ground turmeric
- 1/4 teaspoon saffron threads
- 1 cup chicken broth
- 1 cup diced tomatoes
- 1 cup diced carrots
- 1 cup diced zucchini
- 1 cup diced bell peppers (any color)
- 1 cup green olives, pitted
- Salt and pepper to taste
- Fresh cilantro or parsley, chopped (for garnish)

Instructions:

1. Heat the olive oil in a large tagine or a heavy-bottomed pot over medium heat.
2. Season the chicken thighs with salt and pepper, then add them to the pot, skin side down. Cook until the skin is golden brown and crispy, about 5 minutes. Flip the chicken and cook for an additional 3 minutes. Remove the chicken from the pot and set aside.
3. In the same pot, add the sliced onion and minced garlic. Sauté until the onion becomes translucent and fragrant, about 3-4 minutes.

4. Add the ground cumin, coriander, paprika, turmeric, and saffron threads to the pot. Stir well to coat the onions and garlic with the spices.
5. Pour in the chicken broth and diced tomatoes, scraping the bottom of the pot to release any browned bits. Bring the mixture to a simmer.
6. Return the chicken thighs to the pot, along with the diced carrots, zucchini, bell peppers, and green olives. Stir to combine all the Ingredients.
7. Cover the pot and reduce the heat to low. Allow the tagine to simmer for 1 hour, or until the chicken is cooked through and the vegetables are tender.
8. Taste and adjust the seasoning with salt and pepper if needed.
9. Serve the Chicken and Vegetable Tagine with Saffron hot, garnished with fresh cilantro or parsley.

Nutrition information (per serving):
- Calories: 380
- Fat: 20g
- Carbohydrates: 20g
- Protein: 30g
- Fiber: 5g

28. Beef and Sweet Potato Tagine

Beef and Sweet Potato Tagine is a delicious and hearty Moroccan dish that combines tender beef, sweet potatoes, and aromatic spices. This slow-cooked stew is perfect for chilly evenings and will fill your home with mouthwatering aromas. Serve it with couscous or crusty bread for a complete and satisfying meal.
Serving: 4 servings
Preparation time: 15 minutes
Ready time: 2 hours 30 minutes

Ingredients:
- 1.5 pounds beef stew meat, cut into cubes
- 2 tablespoons olive oil
- 1 onion, diced
- 3 cloves garlic, minced
- 2 teaspoons ground cumin

- 1 teaspoon ground coriander
- 1 teaspoon ground cinnamon
- 1 teaspoon paprika
- 1/2 teaspoon ground ginger
- 1/4 teaspoon cayenne pepper (optional, for heat)
- 2 cups beef broth
- 1 can (14 ounces) diced tomatoes
- 2 medium sweet potatoes, peeled and cut into chunks
- 1/2 cup pitted green olives
- Salt and pepper, to taste
- Fresh cilantro, chopped (for garnish)

Instructions:
1. In a large pot or Dutch oven, heat the olive oil over medium heat. Add the beef cubes and brown them on all sides. Remove the beef from the pot and set aside.
2. In the same pot, add the diced onion and minced garlic. Sauté until the onion becomes translucent and fragrant.
3. Add the ground cumin, ground coriander, ground cinnamon, paprika, ground ginger, and cayenne pepper (if using) to the pot. Stir well to coat the onions and garlic with the spices.
4. Return the browned beef cubes to the pot and mix them with the onion and spice mixture.
5. Pour in the beef broth and diced tomatoes (with their juices). Stir to combine everything.
6. Bring the mixture to a boil, then reduce the heat to low. Cover the pot and let it simmer for 1 hour, stirring occasionally.
7. After 1 hour, add the sweet potato chunks and green olives to the pot. Season with salt and pepper to taste. Stir well.
8. Cover the pot again and continue simmering for another 1 hour, or until the beef is tender and the sweet potatoes are cooked through.
9. Once the beef and sweet potatoes are tender, remove the pot from the heat. Let it rest for a few minutes before serving.
10. Serve the Beef and Sweet Potato Tagine hot, garnished with fresh chopped cilantro. Enjoy with couscous or crusty bread.

Nutrition information per Serving: - Calories: 420
- Fat: 18g
- Carbohydrates: 32g
- Protein: 34g

- Fiber: 6g
- Sugar: 8g
- Sodium: 780mg

29. Fish Tagine with Ginger and Cilantro

Fish Tagine with Ginger and Cilantro is a flavorful and aromatic dish that combines the delicate taste of fish with the bold flavors of ginger and cilantro. This Moroccan-inspired recipe is perfect for a special dinner or a weekend meal with family and friends. The combination of spices and herbs creates a tantalizing aroma that will fill your kitchen and leave your taste buds wanting more.
Serving: 4 servings
Preparation time: 15 minutes
Ready time: 45 minutes

Ingredients:
- 4 fish fillets (such as cod, halibut, or sea bass)
- 2 tablespoons olive oil
- 1 onion, finely chopped
- 3 cloves of garlic, minced
- 1 tablespoon grated fresh ginger
- 1 teaspoon ground cumin
- 1 teaspoon ground coriander
- 1 teaspoon paprika
- 1/2 teaspoon ground turmeric
- 1/4 teaspoon cayenne pepper (optional, for heat)
- 1 can (14 ounces) diced tomatoes
- 1/2 cup vegetable or fish broth
- 1/4 cup chopped fresh cilantro
- Salt and pepper to taste
- Lemon wedges, for Serving:

Instructions:
1. Preheat your oven to 375°F (190°C).
2. In a large oven-safe skillet or tagine, heat the olive oil over medium heat. Add the chopped onion and cook until softened, about 5 minutes.

3. Add the minced garlic and grated ginger to the skillet and cook for an additional 1-2 minutes, until fragrant.
4. In a small bowl, combine the ground cumin, coriander, paprika, turmeric, and cayenne pepper (if using). Stir the spice mixture into the skillet and cook for another minute to toast the spices.
5. Pour in the diced tomatoes and vegetable or fish broth. Bring the mixture to a simmer and let it cook for 5 minutes, allowing the flavors to meld together.
6. Season the fish fillets with salt and pepper, then nestle them into the tomato mixture in the skillet. Spoon some of the sauce over the fish.
7. Cover the skillet or tagine with a lid or aluminum foil and transfer it to the preheated oven. Bake for 20-25 minutes, or until the fish is cooked through and flakes easily with a fork.
8. Remove the skillet from the oven and sprinkle the chopped cilantro over the fish. Serve the Fish Tagine with Ginger and Cilantro hot, with lemon wedges on the side for squeezing over the fish.

Nutrition information:
- Calories: 250 per Serving: - Fat: 10g
- Carbohydrates: 10g
- Protein: 30g
- Fiber: 3g
- Sodium: 400mg

30. Moroccan Chicken Tagine with Chickpeas and Zucchini

Moroccan Chicken Tagine with Chickpeas and Zucchini is a flavorful and aromatic dish that combines tender chicken, hearty chickpeas, and fresh zucchini in a rich and fragrant sauce. This traditional Moroccan recipe is perfect for those looking to explore the vibrant flavors of North African cuisine. With a blend of spices and slow cooking, this dish is sure to transport your taste buds to the bustling streets of Morocco.
Serving: 4 servings
Preparation time: 15 minutes
Ready time: 1 hour 30 minutes

Ingredients:

- 4 chicken thighs, bone-in and skin-on
- 1 tablespoon olive oil
- 1 onion, finely chopped
- 3 cloves of garlic, minced
- 1 teaspoon ground cumin
- 1 teaspoon ground coriander
- 1 teaspoon ground paprika
- 1 teaspoon ground turmeric
- 1 teaspoon ground cinnamon
- 1/2 teaspoon ground ginger
- 1/4 teaspoon cayenne pepper (optional, for heat)
- 1 can (14 ounces) diced tomatoes
- 1 can (14 ounces) chickpeas, drained and rinsed
- 2 zucchinis, sliced into rounds
- 1/2 cup chicken broth
- Salt and pepper to taste
- Fresh cilantro or parsley, chopped (for garnish)

Instructions:

1. Heat the olive oil in a large, heavy-bottomed pot or tagine over medium heat. Add the chicken thighs, skin-side down, and cook until browned and crispy, about 5 minutes per side. Remove the chicken from the pot and set aside.
2. In the same pot, add the chopped onion and minced garlic. Sauté until the onion becomes translucent and fragrant, about 5 minutes.
3. Add the ground cumin, coriander, paprika, turmeric, cinnamon, ginger, and cayenne pepper (if using) to the pot. Stir well to coat the onions and garlic with the spices.
4. Pour in the diced tomatoes and chicken broth, and bring the mixture to a simmer. Return the chicken thighs to the pot, along with any accumulated juices. Season with salt and pepper to taste.
5. Cover the pot and let the chicken simmer over low heat for 1 hour, or until the meat is tender and easily falls off the bone.
6. Add the drained and rinsed chickpeas and sliced zucchini to the pot. Stir gently to combine. Cover the pot again and continue to simmer for an additional 15 minutes, or until the zucchini is cooked through but still slightly firm.
7. Taste and adjust the seasoning if needed. If the sauce is too thin, simmer uncovered for a few more minutes to thicken it slightly.

8. Serve the Moroccan Chicken Tagine with Chickpeas and Zucchini hot, garnished with fresh cilantro or parsley. This dish pairs well with couscous or crusty bread.

Nutrition information:
- Calories: 380
- Fat: 18g
- Carbohydrates: 25g
- Protein: 30g
- Fiber: 6g
- Sugar: 6g
- Sodium: 480mg

31. Lamb and Artichoke Tagine

Lamb and Artichoke Tagine is a flavorful and aromatic Moroccan dish that combines tender lamb with artichokes and a blend of spices. This slow-cooked stew is perfect for a cozy dinner and will transport you to the vibrant streets of Morocco with its rich flavors.
Serving: 4 servings
Preparation time: 20 minutes
Ready time: 2 hours 30 minutes

Ingredients:
- 1.5 pounds lamb shoulder, cut into chunks
- 1 onion, finely chopped
- 3 cloves of garlic, minced
- 1 teaspoon ground cumin
- 1 teaspoon ground coriander
- 1 teaspoon ground turmeric
- 1 teaspoon ground cinnamon
- 1 teaspoon paprika
- 1/2 teaspoon ground ginger
- 1/4 teaspoon cayenne pepper (optional, for heat)
- 1 can (14 ounces) artichoke hearts, drained and quartered
- 1 cup chicken broth
- 1 tablespoon honey
- 2 tablespoons olive oil

- Salt and pepper to taste
- Fresh cilantro, chopped (for garnish)

Instructions:

1. In a large tagine or a heavy-bottomed pot, heat the olive oil over medium heat. Add the lamb chunks and brown them on all sides. Remove the lamb from the pot and set aside.
2. In the same pot, add the chopped onion and minced garlic. Sauté until the onion becomes translucent and fragrant.
3. Add the ground cumin, coriander, turmeric, cinnamon, paprika, ginger, and cayenne pepper (if using) to the pot. Stir well to coat the onions and garlic with the spices.
4. Return the browned lamb to the pot and mix it with the onion and spice mixture. Season with salt and pepper to taste.
5. Pour in the chicken broth and bring the mixture to a simmer. Cover the pot and let it cook on low heat for about 2 hours, or until the lamb becomes tender and starts to fall apart.
6. Add the quartered artichoke hearts and honey to the pot. Stir gently to combine all the Ingredients. Cover the pot again and let it cook for an additional 15-20 minutes, or until the artichokes are heated through.
7. Taste and adjust the seasoning if needed. If the sauce is too thin, you can simmer it uncovered for a few more minutes to thicken it slightly.
8. Serve the Lamb and Artichoke Tagine hot, garnished with fresh chopped cilantro. It pairs well with couscous or crusty bread.

Nutrition information (per serving):

- Calories: 420
- Fat: 22g
- Carbohydrates: 18g
- Protein: 38g
- Fiber: 6g
- Sugar: 6g
- Sodium: 680mg

32. Vegetable Tagine with Spiced Tomato Sauce

Vegetable Tagine with Spiced Tomato Sauce is a delicious and healthy dish that is packed with flavors. This Moroccan-inspired recipe combines

a variety of vegetables with a fragrant spiced tomato sauce, resulting in a hearty and satisfying meal. Whether you are a vegetarian or simply looking to incorporate more vegetables into your diet, this dish is sure to impress.
Serving: 4 servings
Preparation time: 15 minutes
Ready time: 1 hour

Ingredients:
- 2 tablespoons olive oil
- 1 onion, diced
- 3 cloves of garlic, minced
- 1 teaspoon ground cumin
- 1 teaspoon ground coriander
- 1 teaspoon ground paprika
- 1/2 teaspoon ground turmeric
- 1/4 teaspoon ground cinnamon
- 1/4 teaspoon cayenne pepper (optional, for heat)
- 1 can (400g) diced tomatoes
- 1 cup vegetable broth
- 1 sweet potato, peeled and diced
- 2 carrots, peeled and sliced
- 1 zucchini, sliced
- 1 red bell pepper, diced
- 1 cup cooked chickpeas
- Salt and pepper to taste
- Fresh cilantro or parsley, for garnish

Instructions:
1. Heat the olive oil in a large pot or tagine over medium heat. Add the diced onion and minced garlic, and sauté until the onion becomes translucent and fragrant.
2. In a small bowl, combine the ground cumin, coriander, paprika, turmeric, cinnamon, and cayenne pepper. Stir well to create a spice blend.
3. Add the spice blend to the pot and cook for an additional minute, stirring constantly to coat the onions and garlic.
4. Pour in the diced tomatoes and vegetable broth, and bring the mixture to a simmer. Allow it to cook for about 10 minutes, allowing the flavors to meld together.

5. Add the diced sweet potato, sliced carrots, zucchini, red bell pepper, and cooked chickpeas to the pot. Stir well to combine all the Ingredients.
6. Cover the pot and let the tagine simmer for about 40-45 minutes, or until the vegetables are tender.
7. Season with salt and pepper to taste. If desired, adjust the spice level by adding more cayenne pepper.
8. Serve the Vegetable Tagine with Spiced Tomato Sauce hot, garnished with fresh cilantro or parsley. It pairs well with couscous or crusty bread.

Nutrition information per Serving: - Calories: 250
- Fat: 8g
- Carbohydrates: 40g
- Fiber: 10g
- Protein: 8g
- Sodium: 500mg

33. Spicy Harissa Beef Tagine

Spicy Harissa Beef Tagine is a flavorful and aromatic Moroccan dish that combines tender beef with a spicy and tangy harissa sauce. This dish is perfect for those who enjoy a bit of heat in their meals. The slow cooking process allows the flavors to meld together, resulting in a rich and satisfying meal. Serve this tagine with couscous or warm crusty bread for a complete and delicious meal.
Serving: 4 servings
Preparation time: 15 minutes
Ready time: 2 hours 30 minutes

Ingredients:
- 1.5 pounds beef stew meat, cut into chunks
- 2 tablespoons olive oil
- 1 onion, diced
- 3 cloves garlic, minced
- 2 tablespoons harissa paste
- 1 teaspoon ground cumin
- 1 teaspoon ground coriander
- 1 teaspoon ground paprika
- 1 teaspoon ground turmeric

- 1 teaspoon salt
- 1/2 teaspoon black pepper
- 1 cup beef broth
- 1 can (14 ounces) diced tomatoes
- 1 tablespoon honey
- 1 tablespoon lemon juice
- Fresh cilantro, chopped (for garnish)

Instructions:

1. In a large pot or tagine, heat the olive oil over medium heat. Add the beef chunks and brown them on all sides. Remove the beef from the pot and set aside.
2. In the same pot, add the diced onion and minced garlic. Sauté until the onion becomes translucent and fragrant.
3. Add the harissa paste, cumin, coriander, paprika, turmeric, salt, and black pepper to the pot. Stir well to coat the onions and garlic with the spices.
4. Return the browned beef to the pot and mix it with the spiced onion mixture.
5. Pour in the beef broth and diced tomatoes, including their juices. Stir in the honey and lemon juice.
6. Bring the mixture to a boil, then reduce the heat to low. Cover the pot and let it simmer for about 2 hours, or until the beef is tender and the flavors have melded together.
7. Once the beef is tender, taste the tagine and adjust the seasoning if needed.
8. Serve the Spicy Harissa Beef Tagine hot, garnished with fresh chopped cilantro. It pairs well with couscous or warm crusty bread.

Nutrition information (per serving):

- Calories: 380
- Fat: 18g
- Carbohydrates: 15g
- Protein: 38g
- Fiber: 3g
- Sugar: 8g
- Sodium: 900mg

34. Moroccan Meatball Tagine with Tomato Sauce

Moroccan Meatball Tagine with Tomato Sauce is a flavorful and aromatic dish that combines tender meatballs with a rich tomato sauce. This traditional Moroccan recipe is packed with spices and herbs, creating a delicious and satisfying meal. Serve it with couscous or crusty bread for a complete and hearty dinner.
Serving: 4 servings
Preparation time: 20 minutes
Ready time: 1 hour 10 minutes

Ingredients:
- 500g ground beef or lamb
- 1 small onion, finely chopped
- 2 cloves of garlic, minced
- 1 teaspoon ground cumin
- 1 teaspoon ground coriander
- 1 teaspoon paprika
- 1/2 teaspoon ground cinnamon
- 1/2 teaspoon ground ginger
- 1/4 teaspoon cayenne pepper (optional, for heat)
- Salt and pepper to taste
- 2 tablespoons olive oil
- 1 can (400g) diced tomatoes
- 1 tablespoon tomato paste
- 1 cup beef or vegetable broth
- 1 tablespoon honey
- Fresh cilantro or parsley, chopped (for garnish)

Instructions:
1. In a large bowl, combine the ground meat, chopped onion, minced garlic, cumin, coriander, paprika, cinnamon, ginger, cayenne pepper (if using), salt, and pepper. Mix well until all the Ingredients are evenly incorporated.
2. Shape the meat mixture into small meatballs, about 1 inch in diameter.
3. Heat the olive oil in a large tagine or a deep skillet over medium heat. Add the meatballs and cook until browned on all sides, about 5 minutes. Remove the meatballs from the tagine and set aside.
4. In the same tagine or skillet, add the diced tomatoes, tomato paste, beef or vegetable broth, and honey. Stir well to combine.

5. Return the meatballs to the tagine, making sure they are submerged in the tomato sauce. Cover and simmer over low heat for 45 minutes to 1 hour, or until the meatballs are cooked through and tender.
6. Serve the Moroccan Meatball Tagine with Tomato Sauce hot, garnished with fresh cilantro or parsley. It pairs well with couscous or crusty bread.

Nutrition information per Serving: - Calories: 350
- Fat: 20g
- Carbohydrates: 15g
- Protein: 25g
- Fiber: 3g
- Sugar: 8g
- Sodium: 600mg

35. Chicken and Prune Tagine

Chicken and Prune Tagine is a delicious Moroccan dish that combines tender chicken with sweet prunes and aromatic spices. This slow-cooked stew is bursting with flavors and is perfect for a cozy family dinner or a special occasion. The combination of savory and sweet flavors in this dish will surely leave you wanting more.
Serving: 4 servings
Preparation time: 15 minutes
Ready time: 1 hour 30 minutes

Ingredients:
- 4 chicken thighs, bone-in and skin-on
- 1 onion, finely chopped
- 3 cloves of garlic, minced
- 1 teaspoon ground cumin
- 1 teaspoon ground ginger
- 1 teaspoon ground cinnamon
- 1/2 teaspoon ground turmeric
- 1/2 teaspoon ground coriander
- 1/4 teaspoon cayenne pepper (optional, for heat)
- 1 cup pitted prunes
- 1 cup chicken broth

- 2 tablespoons olive oil
- Salt and pepper to taste
- Fresh cilantro or parsley, chopped (for garnish)

Instructions:

1. In a large tagine or a heavy-bottomed pot, heat the olive oil over medium heat. Add the chicken thighs, skin-side down, and cook until browned, about 5 minutes. Flip the chicken and brown the other side for an additional 5 minutes. Remove the chicken from the pot and set aside.
2. In the same pot, add the chopped onion and minced garlic. Sauté until the onion becomes translucent and the garlic is fragrant, about 3 minutes.
3. Add the ground cumin, ginger, cinnamon, turmeric, coriander, and cayenne pepper (if using) to the pot. Stir well to coat the onions and garlic with the spices.
4. Return the chicken thighs to the pot, along with any juices that may have accumulated. Add the pitted prunes and chicken broth. Season with salt and pepper to taste.
5. Bring the mixture to a boil, then reduce the heat to low. Cover the pot and simmer for 1 hour, or until the chicken is tender and cooked through.
6. Once the chicken is cooked, remove it from the pot and set aside. Increase the heat to medium-high and simmer the sauce uncovered for about 10 minutes, or until it thickens slightly.
7. Return the chicken to the pot and cook for an additional 5 minutes to allow the flavors to meld together.
8. Serve the Chicken and Prune Tagine hot, garnished with fresh cilantro or parsley. It pairs well with couscous or crusty bread.

Nutrition information:

- Calories: 380
- Fat: 18g
- Carbohydrates: 25g
- Protein: 30g
- Fiber: 4g
- Sodium: 450mg

36. Vegetable and Lentil Tagine

Vegetable and Lentil Tagine is a delicious and nutritious dish that combines the flavors of various vegetables and lentils with aromatic spices. This Moroccan-inspired dish is not only packed with flavor but also provides a good source of protein and fiber. It is a perfect option for a healthy and satisfying meal.
Serving: 4 servings
Preparation time: 15 minutes
Ready time: 1 hour

Ingredients:
- 1 tablespoon olive oil
- 1 onion, diced
- 2 cloves of garlic, minced
- 1 teaspoon ground cumin
- 1 teaspoon ground coriander
- 1 teaspoon ground turmeric
- 1 teaspoon paprika
- 1 teaspoon ground cinnamon
- 1 cup dried lentils, rinsed and drained
- 2 carrots, peeled and sliced
- 2 zucchinis, sliced
- 1 red bell pepper, diced
- 1 can (14 oz) diced tomatoes
- 2 cups vegetable broth
- Salt and pepper to taste
- Fresh cilantro or parsley, chopped (for garnish)

Instructions:
1. Heat the olive oil in a large pot or tagine over medium heat. Add the diced onion and minced garlic, and sauté until they become translucent and fragrant.
2. Add the ground cumin, coriander, turmeric, paprika, and cinnamon to the pot. Stir well to coat the onions and garlic with the spices.
3. Add the rinsed lentils, sliced carrots, zucchinis, and diced red bell pepper to the pot. Stir everything together to combine.
4. Pour in the diced tomatoes and vegetable broth. Season with salt and pepper to taste.

5. Bring the mixture to a boil, then reduce the heat to low. Cover the pot and let it simmer for about 45 minutes to 1 hour, or until the lentils and vegetables are tender.
6. Once cooked, remove the tagine from the heat and let it sit for a few minutes before serving.
7. Garnish with fresh cilantro or parsley before serving.

Nutrition information per Serving: - Calories: 250
- Protein: 12g
- Fat: 4g
- Carbohydrates: 45g
- Fiber: 12g
- Sugar: 8g
- Sodium: 600mg

Note: Nutrition information may vary depending on the specific Ingredients and brands used.

37. Fish Tagine with Cumin and Paprika

Fish Tagine with Cumin and Paprika is a delicious and aromatic Moroccan dish that combines the flavors of cumin, paprika, and fresh fish. This dish is perfect for seafood lovers and those who enjoy the rich and exotic flavors of Moroccan cuisine. The tagine cooking method ensures that the fish remains tender and moist, while the spices infuse the dish with a delightful warmth. Serve this Fish Tagine with Cumin and Paprika with couscous or crusty bread for a complete and satisfying meal.
Serving: 4 servings
Preparation time: 15 minutes
Ready time: 45 minutes

Ingredients:
- 4 fish fillets (such as cod, haddock, or sea bass)
- 2 tablespoons olive oil
- 1 onion, finely chopped
- 3 garlic cloves, minced
- 1 teaspoon ground cumin
- 1 teaspoon paprika

- 1 teaspoon ground coriander
- 1 teaspoon ground ginger
- 1 teaspoon salt
- 1/2 teaspoon black pepper
- 1 can (400g) diced tomatoes
- 1/2 cup vegetable or fish broth
- 1 tablespoon lemon juice
- Fresh cilantro or parsley, chopped (for garnish)

Instructions:
1. Preheat your oven to 375°F (190°C).
2. In a large oven-safe skillet or tagine, heat the olive oil over medium heat.
3. Add the chopped onion and minced garlic to the skillet and sauté until they become translucent and fragrant, about 5 minutes.
4. In a small bowl, mix together the ground cumin, paprika, coriander, ginger, salt, and black pepper.
5. Sprinkle the spice mixture evenly over both sides of the fish fillets.
6. Place the seasoned fish fillets on top of the sautéed onions and garlic in the skillet.
7. Pour the diced tomatoes, vegetable or fish broth, and lemon juice over the fish.
8. Cover the skillet or tagine with a lid or aluminum foil and transfer it to the preheated oven.
9. Bake for 25-30 minutes, or until the fish is cooked through and flakes easily with a fork.
10. Remove the skillet from the oven and garnish with fresh cilantro or parsley.
11. Serve the Fish Tagine with Cumin and Paprika hot with couscous or crusty bread.

Nutrition information:
- Calories: 250
- Fat: 10g
- Carbohydrates: 10g
- Protein: 30g
- Fiber: 2g
- Sodium: 600mg

38. Moroccan Chicken Tagine with Carrots and Potatoes

Moroccan Chicken Tagine with Carrots and Potatoes is a flavorful and aromatic dish that combines tender chicken with a medley of vegetables and traditional Moroccan spices. This hearty and comforting meal is perfect for a family dinner or for entertaining guests. The slow cooking process allows the flavors to meld together, resulting in a dish that is both delicious and satisfying.
Serving: 4 servings
Preparation time: 15 minutes
Ready time: 1 hour 30 minutes

Ingredients:
- 4 chicken thighs, bone-in and skin-on
- 2 tablespoons olive oil
- 1 onion, finely chopped
- 3 cloves of garlic, minced
- 2 teaspoons ground cumin
- 2 teaspoons ground coriander
- 1 teaspoon ground turmeric
- 1 teaspoon ground cinnamon
- 1 teaspoon paprika
- 1 teaspoon salt
- 1/2 teaspoon black pepper
- 4 carrots, peeled and cut into chunks
- 2 potatoes, peeled and cut into chunks
- 1 cup chicken broth
- 1/4 cup chopped fresh cilantro (optional, for garnish)

Instructions:
1. Heat the olive oil in a large, heavy-bottomed pot or tagine over medium heat. Add the chicken thighs, skin-side down, and cook until browned, about 5 minutes. Flip the chicken and brown the other side for an additional 5 minutes. Remove the chicken from the pot and set aside.
2. In the same pot, add the chopped onion and minced garlic. Sauté until the onion is translucent and fragrant, about 5 minutes.

3. Add the ground cumin, ground coriander, ground turmeric, ground cinnamon, paprika, salt, and black pepper to the pot. Stir well to coat the onions and garlic with the spices.
4. Return the chicken thighs to the pot, along with any accumulated juices. Add the carrots and potatoes to the pot, arranging them around the chicken.
5. Pour the chicken broth over the chicken and vegetables. Bring the mixture to a simmer, then reduce the heat to low. Cover the pot and let it cook for 1 hour, or until the chicken is cooked through and the vegetables are tender.
6. Once cooked, remove the chicken thighs from the pot and set aside. Increase the heat to medium-high and let the sauce reduce for about 5 minutes, or until slightly thickened.
7. Serve the Moroccan Chicken Tagine with Carrots and Potatoes hot, garnished with chopped fresh cilantro if desired. It pairs well with couscous or crusty bread.

Nutrition information (per serving):
- Calories: 380
- Fat: 18g
- Carbohydrates: 25g
- Protein: 28g
- Fiber: 5g
- Sugar: 5g
- Sodium: 800mg

39. Lamb and Fig Tagine

Lamb and Fig Tagine is a delicious and aromatic Moroccan dish that combines tender lamb with sweet and tangy figs. This slow-cooked stew is packed with flavors from a blend of spices and is perfect for a cozy dinner or special occasion. The combination of tender meat and succulent figs creates a harmony of flavors that will leave your taste buds wanting more.
Serving: 4 servings
Preparation time: 20 minutes
Ready time: 2 hours 30 minutes

Ingredients:

- 1.5 pounds lamb shoulder, cut into chunks
- 1 onion, finely chopped
- 3 cloves of garlic, minced
- 1 teaspoon ground cumin
- 1 teaspoon ground coriander
- 1 teaspoon ground cinnamon
- 1 teaspoon ground ginger
- 1/2 teaspoon ground turmeric
- 1/2 teaspoon paprika
- 1/4 teaspoon cayenne pepper (optional, for heat)
- 1 cup dried figs, halved
- 2 tablespoons honey
- 2 cups chicken or vegetable broth
- 2 tablespoons olive oil
- Salt and pepper to taste
- Fresh cilantro or parsley, chopped (for garnish)

Instructions:

1. In a large tagine or heavy-bottomed pot, heat the olive oil over medium heat. Add the lamb chunks and brown them on all sides. Remove the lamb from the pot and set aside.
2. In the same pot, add the chopped onion and minced garlic. Sauté until the onion becomes translucent and fragrant.
3. Add the ground cumin, coriander, cinnamon, ginger, turmeric, paprika, and cayenne pepper (if using) to the pot. Stir well to coat the onions and garlic with the spices.
4. Return the browned lamb to the pot and mix it with the onion and spice mixture. Season with salt and pepper to taste.
5. Pour in the chicken or vegetable broth, ensuring that the meat is fully covered. Bring the mixture to a boil, then reduce the heat to low and cover the pot. Let it simmer for about 2 hours, or until the lamb is tender and easily falls apart.
6. Add the dried figs and honey to the pot, stirring gently to combine. Cover the pot again and let it simmer for an additional 30 minutes, allowing the flavors to meld together.
7. Once the lamb is tender and the figs have softened, remove the pot from the heat. Let it rest for a few minutes before serving.
8. Serve the Lamb and Fig Tagine hot, garnished with fresh cilantro or parsley. It pairs well with couscous or crusty bread.

Nutrition information:
- Calories: 420 per Serving: - Fat: 18g
- Carbohydrates: 32g
- Protein: 34g
- Fiber: 6g
- Sugar: 23g
- Sodium: 650mg

40. Vegetable Tagine with Chickpeas and Dates

Vegetable Tagine with Chickpeas and Dates is a delicious and hearty Moroccan-inspired dish that combines a medley of vegetables, protein-rich chickpeas, and sweet dates. This flavorful tagine is packed with nutrients and is perfect for a comforting and satisfying meal.
Serving: 4 servings
Preparation time: 15 minutes
Ready time: 1 hour

Ingredients:
- 2 tablespoons olive oil
- 1 onion, diced
- 3 cloves of garlic, minced
- 1 teaspoon ground cumin
- 1 teaspoon ground coriander
- 1 teaspoon ground turmeric
- 1 teaspoon ground cinnamon
- 1 teaspoon paprika
- 1 teaspoon salt
- 1/2 teaspoon black pepper
- 1 cup diced carrots
- 1 cup diced bell peppers (any color)
- 1 cup diced zucchini
- 1 cup diced eggplant
- 1 can (15 ounces) chickpeas, drained and rinsed
- 1 cup pitted dates, chopped
- 1 can (14 ounces) diced tomatoes
- 1 cup vegetable broth

- Fresh cilantro or parsley, for garnish (optional)

Instructions:

1. Heat the olive oil in a large pot or tagine over medium heat. Add the diced onion and minced garlic, and sauté until the onion becomes translucent and fragrant.
2. Add the ground cumin, coriander, turmeric, cinnamon, paprika, salt, and black pepper to the pot. Stir well to coat the onions and garlic with the spices.
3. Add the diced carrots, bell peppers, zucchini, and eggplant to the pot. Stir to combine the vegetables with the spices.
4. Add the drained chickpeas, chopped dates, diced tomatoes, and vegetable broth to the pot. Stir everything together.
5. Bring the mixture to a boil, then reduce the heat to low. Cover the pot and let it simmer for about 45 minutes to 1 hour, or until the vegetables are tender and the flavors have melded together.
6. Taste and adjust the seasoning if needed.
7. Serve the Vegetable Tagine with Chickpeas and Dates hot, garnished with fresh cilantro or parsley if desired. It pairs well with couscous or crusty bread.

Nutrition information per Serving: - Calories: 320

- Fat: 8g
- Carbohydrates: 55g
- Fiber: 12g
- Protein: 10g
- Sodium: 800mg

41. Spicy Harissa Lamb Tagine

Spicy Harissa Lamb Tagine is a flavorful and aromatic Moroccan dish that combines tender lamb with a spicy harissa sauce and a medley of vegetables. This dish is perfect for those who enjoy a bit of heat and a burst of exotic flavors. The slow cooking process allows the flavors to meld together, resulting in a rich and satisfying meal.

Serving: 4 servings

Preparation time: 20 minutes

Ready time: 2 hours 30 minutes

Ingredients:
- 1.5 pounds lamb shoulder, cut into chunks
- 2 tablespoons olive oil
- 1 onion, finely chopped
- 3 cloves of garlic, minced
- 2 tablespoons harissa paste
- 1 teaspoon ground cumin
- 1 teaspoon ground coriander
- 1 teaspoon ground cinnamon
- 1 teaspoon paprika
- 1 teaspoon salt
- 1/2 teaspoon black pepper
- 1 cup diced tomatoes
- 2 cups chicken or vegetable broth
- 1 cup chopped carrots
- 1 cup chopped bell peppers
- 1 cup chopped zucchini
- 1/2 cup pitted green olives
- Fresh cilantro, for garnish

Instructions:
1. Heat the olive oil in a large tagine or a heavy-bottomed pot over medium heat. Add the lamb chunks and brown them on all sides. Remove the lamb from the pot and set aside.
2. In the same pot, add the chopped onion and minced garlic. Sauté until the onion becomes translucent and fragrant.
3. Add the harissa paste, ground cumin, ground coriander, ground cinnamon, paprika, salt, and black pepper to the pot. Stir well to coat the onions and garlic with the spices.
4. Return the browned lamb to the pot and add the diced tomatoes and chicken or vegetable broth. Stir to combine all the Ingredients.
5. Cover the pot and simmer on low heat for 1 hour and 30 minutes, or until the lamb becomes tender.
6. After 1 hour and 30 minutes, add the chopped carrots, bell peppers, zucchini, and green olives to the pot. Stir well and continue to simmer for an additional 30 minutes, or until the vegetables are cooked to your desired tenderness.
7. Serve the Spicy Harissa Lamb Tagine hot, garnished with fresh cilantro. This dish pairs well with couscous or crusty bread.

Nutrition information:
- Calories: 420
- Fat: 22g
- Carbohydrates: 15g
- Protein: 38g
- Fiber: 4g
- Sodium: 950mg

42. Moroccan Meatball Tagine with Peppers

Moroccan Meatball Tagine with Peppers is a flavorful and aromatic dish that combines tender meatballs with a rich tomato and pepper sauce. This traditional Moroccan recipe is packed with spices and herbs, creating a dish that is both comforting and exotic. Serve it with couscous or crusty bread for a complete and satisfying meal.
Serving: 4 servings
Preparation time: 20 minutes
Ready time: 1 hour 10 minutes

Ingredients:
- 500g ground beef or lamb
- 1 onion, finely chopped
- 3 cloves of garlic, minced
- 1 teaspoon ground cumin
- 1 teaspoon ground coriander
- 1 teaspoon paprika
- 1/2 teaspoon ground cinnamon
- 1/2 teaspoon ground ginger
- 1/4 teaspoon cayenne pepper (optional, for heat)
- Salt and pepper to taste
- 2 tablespoons olive oil
- 1 red bell pepper, sliced
- 1 yellow bell pepper, sliced
- 1 green bell pepper, sliced
- 1 can (400g) diced tomatoes
- 1 cup beef or vegetable broth
- Fresh cilantro or parsley, chopped (for garnish)

Instructions:

1. In a large bowl, combine the ground meat, chopped onion, minced garlic, cumin, coriander, paprika, cinnamon, ginger, cayenne pepper (if using), salt, and pepper. Mix well until all the Ingredients are evenly incorporated.
2. Shape the meat mixture into small meatballs, about 1 inch in diameter.
3. Heat the olive oil in a large, deep skillet or tagine over medium heat. Add the meatballs and cook until browned on all sides, about 5 minutes. Remove the meatballs from the skillet and set aside.
4. In the same skillet, add the sliced bell peppers and cook for 5 minutes, until slightly softened.
5. Return the meatballs to the skillet and add the diced tomatoes and beef or vegetable broth. Stir well to combine.
6. Reduce the heat to low, cover the skillet, and simmer for 45 minutes to 1 hour, until the meatballs are cooked through and the flavors have melded together.
7. Serve the Moroccan Meatball Tagine with Peppers hot, garnished with fresh cilantro or parsley. It pairs perfectly with couscous or crusty bread.

Nutrition information:

- Calories: 350 per Serving: - Fat: 20g
- Carbohydrates: 15g
- Protein: 25g
- Fiber: 4g
- Sodium: 600mg

43. Chicken and Almond Tagine

Chicken and Almond Tagine is a delicious Moroccan dish that combines tender chicken with aromatic spices and crunchy almonds. This flavorful and comforting dish is perfect for a cozy dinner or a special occasion. The slow cooking process allows the flavors to meld together, resulting in a dish that is rich and satisfying. Serve this Chicken and Almond Tagine with couscous or rice for a complete meal that will transport you to the vibrant streets of Morocco.

Serving: 4 servings

Preparation time: 15 minutes

Ready time: 1 hour 30 minutes

Ingredients:
- 4 chicken thighs, bone-in and skin-on
- 1 onion, finely chopped
- 3 cloves of garlic, minced
- 1 teaspoon ground cumin
- 1 teaspoon ground coriander
- 1 teaspoon ground ginger
- 1 teaspoon ground cinnamon
- 1/2 teaspoon ground turmeric
- 1/2 teaspoon paprika
- 1/4 teaspoon cayenne pepper (optional, for heat)
- 1 cup chicken broth
- 1/2 cup dried apricots, chopped
- 1/2 cup green olives, pitted
- 1/4 cup slivered almonds
- 2 tablespoons olive oil
- Salt and pepper to taste
- Fresh cilantro, chopped (for garnish)

Instructions:
1. Season the chicken thighs with salt and pepper. Heat the olive oil in a large tagine or a heavy-bottomed pot over medium-high heat. Brown the chicken thighs on both sides until golden brown. Remove the chicken from the pot and set aside.
2. In the same pot, add the chopped onion and minced garlic. Sauté until the onion becomes translucent and the garlic becomes fragrant.
3. Add the ground cumin, coriander, ginger, cinnamon, turmeric, paprika, and cayenne pepper (if using) to the pot. Stir well to coat the onions and garlic with the spices.
4. Return the chicken thighs to the pot and pour in the chicken broth. Bring the mixture to a simmer, then reduce the heat to low. Cover the pot and let the chicken cook for about 1 hour, or until the meat is tender and cooked through.
5. Add the chopped dried apricots, green olives, and slivered almonds to the pot. Stir gently to combine. Cover the pot again and let the tagine simmer for an additional 15 minutes to allow the flavors to meld together.

6. Taste the tagine and adjust the seasoning with salt and pepper if needed. Garnish with fresh cilantro before serving.

Nutrition information per Serving: - Calories: 380
- Fat: 22g
- Carbohydrates: 17g
- Protein: 28g
- Fiber: 4g
- Sugar: 9g
- Sodium: 620mg

Note: Nutrition information may vary depending on the specific Ingredients and brands used.

44. Vegetable and Quinoa Tagine

Vegetable and Quinoa Tagine is a delicious and nutritious dish that combines the flavors of Moroccan cuisine with the health benefits of vegetables and quinoa. This hearty and filling meal is perfect for vegetarians and vegans, and it can be enjoyed as a main course or a side dish. With its aromatic spices and tender vegetables, this tagine is sure to become a favorite in your household.

Serving: 4 servings

Preparation time: 15 minutes

Ready time: 45 minutes

Ingredients:
- 1 cup quinoa
- 2 tablespoons olive oil
- 1 onion, diced
- 2 cloves garlic, minced
- 1 teaspoon ground cumin
- 1 teaspoon ground coriander
- 1 teaspoon ground turmeric
- 1 teaspoon paprika
- 1 teaspoon cinnamon
- 1 teaspoon salt
- 1 can (14 ounces) diced tomatoes
- 2 cups vegetable broth

- 1 sweet potato, peeled and diced
- 2 carrots, peeled and sliced
- 1 zucchini, sliced
- 1 red bell pepper, diced
- 1 cup chickpeas, drained and rinsed
- 1/4 cup raisins
- Fresh cilantro, for garnish

Instructions:
1. Rinse the quinoa under cold water and drain well.
2. In a large pot, heat the olive oil over medium heat. Add the onion and garlic, and sauté until softened.
3. Add the cumin, coriander, turmeric, paprika, cinnamon, and salt to the pot. Stir well to coat the onions and garlic with the spices.
4. Add the diced tomatoes, vegetable broth, sweet potato, carrots, zucchini, red bell pepper, chickpeas, and raisins to the pot. Stir to combine.
5. Bring the mixture to a boil, then reduce the heat to low. Cover the pot and simmer for 30 minutes, or until the vegetables are tender.
6. While the tagine is simmering, cook the quinoa according to the package instructions.
7. Once the vegetables are tender, remove the tagine from the heat. Serve the vegetable and quinoa tagine over a bed of cooked quinoa.
8. Garnish with fresh cilantro before serving.

Nutrition information per Serving: - Calories: 320
- Fat: 8g
- Carbohydrates: 55g
- Fiber: 10g
- Protein: 10g

45. Fish Tagine with Lemon and Herbs

Fish Tagine with Lemon and Herbs is a delightful Moroccan dish that combines the freshness of fish with the tanginess of lemon and the aromatic flavors of herbs. This dish is not only delicious but also healthy, making it a perfect choice for a light and flavorful meal.
Serving: 4 servings

Preparation time: 15 minutes
Ready time: 45 minutes

Ingredients:
- 4 fish fillets (such as cod, halibut, or sea bass)
- 2 lemons, sliced
- 2 tablespoons olive oil
- 1 onion, finely chopped
- 3 garlic cloves, minced
- 1 teaspoon ground cumin
- 1 teaspoon ground coriander
- 1 teaspoon paprika
- 1 teaspoon turmeric
- 1 teaspoon salt
- 1/2 teaspoon black pepper
- 1 cup vegetable or fish broth
- 1/4 cup fresh cilantro, chopped
- 1/4 cup fresh parsley, chopped

Instructions:
1. Preheat the oven to 375°F (190°C).
2. In a large oven-safe skillet or tagine, heat the olive oil over medium heat. Add the chopped onion and minced garlic, and sauté until they become translucent and fragrant.
3. In a small bowl, mix together the ground cumin, coriander, paprika, turmeric, salt, and black pepper. Sprinkle this spice mixture over the onion and garlic in the skillet, and stir well to coat.
4. Place the fish fillets on top of the onion and spice mixture in the skillet. Arrange the lemon slices on top of the fish.
5. Pour the vegetable or fish broth into the skillet, around the fish fillets. Cover the skillet with a lid or aluminum foil.
6. Transfer the skillet to the preheated oven and bake for about 30 minutes, or until the fish is cooked through and flakes easily with a fork.
7. Once the fish is cooked, remove the skillet from the oven. Sprinkle the chopped cilantro and parsley over the fish.
8. Serve the Fish Tagine with Lemon and Herbs hot, accompanied by couscous or crusty bread.

Nutrition information per Serving: - Calories: 250
- Fat: 10g

- Carbohydrates: 10g
- Protein: 30g
- Fiber: 2g
- Sodium: 600mg

46. Moroccan Chicken Tagine with Pumpkin and Cinnamon

Moroccan Chicken Tagine with Pumpkin and Cinnamon is a flavorful and aromatic dish that combines tender chicken, sweet pumpkin, and warm spices. This traditional Moroccan recipe is perfect for a cozy dinner or a special occasion. The combination of cinnamon, ginger, and cumin adds a unique and exotic flavor to the dish, while the slow cooking process ensures that the chicken is tender and juicy. Serve this delicious tagine with couscous or crusty bread for a complete meal.
Serving: 4 servings
Preparation time: 15 minutes
Ready time: 1 hour 30 minutes

Ingredients:
- 4 chicken thighs, bone-in and skin-on
- 1 small pumpkin, peeled, seeded, and cut into chunks
- 1 onion, finely chopped
- 3 cloves of garlic, minced
- 1 teaspoon ground cinnamon
- 1 teaspoon ground ginger
- 1 teaspoon ground cumin
- 1 teaspoon paprika
- 1 teaspoon salt
- 1/2 teaspoon black pepper
- 2 tablespoons olive oil
- 1 cup chicken broth
- 1/4 cup chopped fresh cilantro (optional, for garnish)

Instructions:
1. In a large bowl, combine the ground cinnamon, ginger, cumin, paprika, salt, and black pepper. Mix well.

2. Add the chicken thighs to the bowl and coat them evenly with the spice mixture. Set aside.
3. Heat the olive oil in a tagine or a large, deep skillet over medium heat.
4. Add the chopped onion and minced garlic to the tagine and sauté until the onion becomes translucent and the garlic becomes fragrant, about 5 minutes.
5. Push the onion and garlic to the sides of the tagine and add the chicken thighs, skin-side down. Cook for 5 minutes, or until the skin is golden brown and crispy.
6. Flip the chicken thighs and add the pumpkin chunks to the tagine. Pour in the chicken broth.
7. Cover the tagine and reduce the heat to low. Simmer for 1 hour, or until the chicken is cooked through and the pumpkin is tender.
8. Remove the tagine from the heat and let it rest for 5 minutes before serving.
9. Garnish with chopped fresh cilantro, if desired.
10. Serve the Moroccan Chicken Tagine with Pumpkin and Cinnamon with couscous or crusty bread.

Nutrition information per Serving: - Calories: 380
- Fat: 20g
- Carbohydrates: 20g
- Protein: 30g
- Fiber: 5g

47. Lamb and Pear Tagine

Lamb and Pear Tagine is a delicious and aromatic Moroccan dish that combines tender lamb with sweet and juicy pears. This slow-cooked stew is packed with warm spices and flavors that will transport you to the vibrant streets of Marrakech. It is the perfect dish to warm you up on a chilly evening or impress your guests at a dinner party.
Serving: 4 servings
Preparation time: 20 minutes
Ready time: 2 hours 30 minutes

Ingredients:
- 1.5 pounds lamb shoulder, cut into chunks

- 2 tablespoons olive oil
- 1 onion, finely chopped
- 3 cloves garlic, minced
- 1 teaspoon ground cumin
- 1 teaspoon ground coriander
- 1 teaspoon ground cinnamon
- 1 teaspoon ground ginger
- 1/2 teaspoon ground turmeric
- 1/2 teaspoon paprika
- 1/4 teaspoon cayenne pepper (optional, for heat)
- 2 ripe pears, peeled, cored, and cut into wedges
- 1 cup chicken or vegetable broth
- 1 tablespoon honey
- 1 tablespoon lemon juice
- Salt and pepper, to taste
- Fresh cilantro, chopped (for garnish)

Instructions:

1. Heat the olive oil in a large, heavy-bottomed pot or tagine over medium heat. Add the lamb chunks and brown them on all sides. Remove the lamb from the pot and set aside.
2. In the same pot, add the chopped onion and minced garlic. Sauté until the onion becomes translucent and fragrant.
3. Add the ground cumin, coriander, cinnamon, ginger, turmeric, paprika, and cayenne pepper (if using) to the pot. Stir well to coat the onions and garlic with the spices.
4. Return the browned lamb to the pot and mix it with the onion and spice mixture. Cook for a few minutes to allow the flavors to meld together.
5. Add the pear wedges, chicken or vegetable broth, honey, and lemon juice to the pot. Stir well to combine all the Ingredients.
6. Bring the mixture to a boil, then reduce the heat to low. Cover the pot and let the tagine simmer for about 2 hours, or until the lamb is tender and the flavors have developed.
7. Season with salt and pepper to taste. If the sauce is too thin, you can remove the lid and simmer for a few more minutes to thicken it.
8. Serve the Lamb and Pear Tagine hot, garnished with fresh chopped cilantro. It pairs well with couscous or crusty bread.

Nutrition information:

- Calories: 380
- Fat: 18g
- Carbohydrates: 25g
- Protein: 30g
- Fiber: 5g
- Sodium: 450mg

48. Vegetable Tagine with Coconut Milk

Vegetable Tagine with Coconut Milk is a delicious and flavorful dish that combines the richness of coconut milk with a medley of vegetables. This Moroccan-inspired recipe is not only easy to make but also packed with nutrients, making it a perfect choice for a healthy and satisfying meal.
Serving: 4 servings
Preparation time: 15 minutes
Ready time: 45 minutes

Ingredients:
- 2 tablespoons olive oil
- 1 onion, diced
- 3 cloves of garlic, minced
- 1 teaspoon ground cumin
- 1 teaspoon ground coriander
- 1 teaspoon ground turmeric
- 1 teaspoon paprika
- 1 teaspoon ground cinnamon
- 1 teaspoon salt
- 1/2 teaspoon black pepper
- 1 can (400ml) coconut milk
- 2 carrots, peeled and sliced
- 1 red bell pepper, sliced
- 1 zucchini, sliced
- 1 cup cauliflower florets
- 1 cup green beans, trimmed
- 1 cup chickpeas, cooked or canned
- 1 cup vegetable broth
- 1 tablespoon fresh cilantro, chopped (for garnish)

Instructions:

1. Heat the olive oil in a large pot or tagine over medium heat. Add the diced onion and minced garlic, and sauté until they become translucent and fragrant.
2. Add the ground cumin, coriander, turmeric, paprika, cinnamon, salt, and black pepper to the pot. Stir well to coat the onions and garlic with the spices.
3. Pour in the coconut milk and stir to combine with the spices. Allow the mixture to simmer for a few minutes to let the flavors meld together.
4. Add the sliced carrots, red bell pepper, zucchini, cauliflower florets, green beans, and chickpeas to the pot. Stir everything together to ensure the vegetables are coated with the coconut milk and spices.
5. Pour in the vegetable broth, cover the pot, and let the tagine simmer for about 30 minutes, or until the vegetables are tender but still retain their shape.
6. Once the vegetables are cooked, remove the pot from the heat. Serve the Vegetable Tagine with Coconut Milk hot, garnished with fresh cilantro.

Nutrition information per Serving: - Calories: 250

- Fat: 15g
- Carbohydrates: 25g
- Fiber: 7g
- Protein: 6g
- Sodium: 600mg

Note: Nutrition information may vary depending on the specific Ingredients and brands used.

49. Spicy Harissa Vegetable Tagine

Spicy Harissa Vegetable Tagine is a flavorful and aromatic Moroccan dish that combines a variety of vegetables with the bold and fiery flavors of harissa paste. This vegetarian tagine is perfect for those who enjoy a bit of heat in their meals and want to explore the rich flavors of North African cuisine. Serve it with couscous or crusty bread for a satisfying and wholesome meal.

Serving: 4 servings

Preparation time: 15 minutes

Ready time: 1 hour

Ingredients:
- 2 tablespoons olive oil
- 1 onion, diced
- 3 garlic cloves, minced
- 2 carrots, peeled and sliced
- 1 red bell pepper, sliced
- 1 yellow bell pepper, sliced
- 1 zucchini, sliced
- 1 eggplant, diced
- 2 tablespoons harissa paste
- 1 teaspoon ground cumin
- 1 teaspoon ground coriander
- 1 teaspoon paprika
- 1 can (400g) diced tomatoes
- 1 cup vegetable broth
- Salt and pepper to taste
- Fresh cilantro, chopped (for garnish)

Instructions:
1. Heat the olive oil in a large tagine or a deep skillet over medium heat.
2. Add the diced onion and minced garlic to the pan and sauté until the onion becomes translucent.
3. Add the sliced carrots, red and yellow bell peppers, zucchini, and diced eggplant to the pan. Stir well to combine.
4. In a small bowl, mix together the harissa paste, ground cumin, ground coriander, and paprika. Add this spice mixture to the pan and stir to coat the vegetables evenly.
5. Pour in the diced tomatoes and vegetable broth. Season with salt and pepper to taste.
6. Cover the tagine or skillet and let it simmer over low heat for about 45 minutes to 1 hour, or until the vegetables are tender.
7. Once cooked, remove from heat and garnish with fresh cilantro.
8. Serve the Spicy Harissa Vegetable Tagine hot with couscous or crusty bread.

Nutrition information:
- Calories: 180
- Fat: 8g

- Carbohydrates: 25g
- Protein: 4g
- Fiber: 7g
- Sodium: 480mg

50. Moroccan Meatball Tagine with Squash

Moroccan Meatball Tagine with Squash is a flavorful and aromatic dish that combines tender meatballs with a rich tomato-based sauce and hearty chunks of squash. This traditional Moroccan recipe is packed with warm spices and is perfect for a cozy family dinner or a gathering with friends. The combination of tender meatballs, sweet squash, and fragrant spices will transport you to the vibrant streets of Morocco.
Serving: 4 servings
Preparation time: 20 minutes
Ready time: 1 hour 20 minutes

Ingredients:
- 1 lb ground beef
- 1 small onion, finely chopped
- 2 cloves of garlic, minced
- 1 teaspoon ground cumin
- 1 teaspoon ground coriander
- 1 teaspoon ground paprika
- 1/2 teaspoon ground cinnamon
- 1/2 teaspoon ground ginger
- 1/4 teaspoon cayenne pepper (optional, for heat)
- Salt and pepper to taste
- 2 tablespoons olive oil
- 1 can (14 oz) diced tomatoes
- 1 cup chicken or vegetable broth
- 1 small butternut squash, peeled, seeded, and cut into chunks
- Fresh cilantro or parsley, chopped (for garnish)

Instructions:
1. In a large bowl, combine the ground beef, chopped onion, minced garlic, ground cumin, ground coriander, ground paprika, ground

cinnamon, ground ginger, cayenne pepper (if using), salt, and pepper. Mix well until all the Ingredients are evenly incorporated.
2. Shape the meat mixture into small meatballs, about 1 inch in diameter.
3. Heat the olive oil in a large tagine or a deep skillet over medium heat. Add the meatballs and cook until browned on all sides, about 5 minutes. Remove the meatballs from the tagine and set aside.
4. In the same tagine, add the diced tomatoes and chicken or vegetable broth. Stir well to combine.
5. Return the meatballs to the tagine and add the chunks of butternut squash. Stir gently to coat the meatballs and squash with the tomato sauce.
6. Cover the tagine and simmer over low heat for about 1 hour, or until the meatballs are cooked through and the squash is tender.
7. Serve the Moroccan Meatball Tagine with Squash hot, garnished with fresh cilantro or parsley. It pairs well with couscous or crusty bread.

Nutrition information per Serving: - Calories: 350
- Fat: 20g
- Carbohydrates: 20g
- Protein: 25g
- Fiber: 5g
- Sugar: 8g
- Sodium: 600mg

51. Chicken and Tomato Tagine

Chicken and Tomato Tagine is a flavorful and aromatic Moroccan dish that combines tender chicken with a rich tomato sauce. This dish is traditionally cooked in a tagine, a clay pot with a conical lid, which helps to infuse the flavors and keep the chicken moist. The combination of spices, tomatoes, and tender chicken makes this dish a crowd-pleaser that is perfect for any occasion.
Serving: 4 servings
Preparation time: 15 minutes
Ready time: 1 hour 30 minutes

Ingredients:
- 4 chicken thighs, bone-in and skin-on

- 2 tablespoons olive oil
- 1 onion, finely chopped
- 3 cloves of garlic, minced
- 1 teaspoon ground cumin
- 1 teaspoon ground coriander
- 1 teaspoon ground paprika
- 1 teaspoon ground turmeric
- 1 teaspoon ground cinnamon
- 1 can (400g) diced tomatoes
- 1 cup chicken broth
- 1 tablespoon honey
- Salt and pepper to taste
- Fresh cilantro, chopped (for garnish)

Instructions:

1. Heat the olive oil in a large tagine or a heavy-bottomed pot over medium heat.
2. Add the chicken thighs, skin-side down, and cook until browned, about 5 minutes. Flip the chicken and brown the other side for an additional 5 minutes. Remove the chicken from the pot and set aside.
3. In the same pot, add the chopped onion and minced garlic. Sauté until the onion becomes translucent, about 5 minutes.
4. Add the ground cumin, coriander, paprika, turmeric, and cinnamon to the pot. Stir well to coat the onions and garlic with the spices.
5. Pour in the diced tomatoes, chicken broth, and honey. Stir to combine all the Ingredients.
6. Return the chicken thighs to the pot, nestling them into the tomato mixture. Season with salt and pepper to taste.
7. Cover the pot with the tagine lid or a tight-fitting lid and reduce the heat to low. Let the chicken simmer for 1 hour, or until the meat is tender and cooked through.
8. Once the chicken is cooked, remove it from the pot and set aside. Increase the heat to medium-high and let the sauce simmer for an additional 10 minutes, or until it thickens slightly.
9. Serve the chicken and tomato tagine hot, garnished with fresh cilantro. It pairs well with couscous or crusty bread.

Nutrition information per Serving: - Calories: 350

- Fat: 20g
- Carbohydrates: 10g

- Protein: 30g
- Fiber: 2g

52. Vegetable and Potato Tagine

Vegetable and Potato Tagine is a delicious and hearty Moroccan dish that is packed with flavors and nutrients. This vegetarian recipe combines a variety of vegetables and potatoes, cooked in a fragrant blend of spices, resulting in a comforting and satisfying meal. Whether you're a vegetarian or simply looking to incorporate more plant-based meals into your diet, this Vegetable and Potato Tagine is sure to become a favorite.
Serving: 4 servings
Preparation time: 15 minutes
Ready time: 1 hour

Ingredients:
- 2 tablespoons olive oil
- 1 onion, diced
- 3 cloves of garlic, minced
- 2 carrots, peeled and sliced
- 2 potatoes, peeled and cubed
- 1 red bell pepper, sliced
- 1 zucchini, sliced
- 1 cup canned chickpeas, drained and rinsed
- 1 can diced tomatoes
- 1 cup vegetable broth
- 1 teaspoon ground cumin
- 1 teaspoon ground coriander
- 1 teaspoon ground turmeric
- 1 teaspoon paprika
- 1/2 teaspoon ground cinnamon
- Salt and pepper to taste
- Fresh cilantro or parsley, chopped (for garnish)

Instructions:
1. Heat the olive oil in a large pot or tagine over medium heat. Add the diced onion and minced garlic, and sauté until the onion becomes translucent and fragrant.

2. Add the sliced carrots, cubed potatoes, red bell pepper, zucchini, and chickpeas to the pot. Stir well to combine all the vegetables.
3. Pour in the diced tomatoes and vegetable broth. Stir in the ground cumin, coriander, turmeric, paprika, and cinnamon. Season with salt and pepper to taste.
4. Bring the mixture to a boil, then reduce the heat to low. Cover the pot and let it simmer for about 45 minutes to 1 hour, or until the vegetables are tender and the flavors have melded together.
5. Once cooked, remove the pot from the heat and let it sit for a few minutes before serving.
6. Serve the Vegetable and Potato Tagine hot, garnished with fresh cilantro or parsley. It pairs well with couscous or crusty bread.

Nutrition information per Serving: - Calories: 250
- Fat: 8g
- Carbohydrates: 40g
- Fiber: 10g
- Protein: 8g
- Sodium: 500mg

Note: Nutrition information may vary depending on the specific Ingredients and brands used.

53. Fish Tagine with Green Olives and Lemon

Fish Tagine with Green Olives and Lemon is a delicious and aromatic Moroccan dish that combines the flavors of tender fish, tangy green olives, and zesty lemon. This dish is cooked in a traditional tagine, which helps to infuse the fish with all the wonderful spices and Ingredients. It is a perfect dish to impress your guests or to enjoy with your family on a special occasion.
Serving: 4 servings
Preparation time: 15 minutes
Ready time: 45 minutes

Ingredients:
- 4 fish fillets (such as cod, halibut, or sea bass)
- 1 onion, finely chopped
- 2 cloves of garlic, minced

- 1 teaspoon ground cumin
- 1 teaspoon ground coriander
- 1 teaspoon paprika
- 1/2 teaspoon ground turmeric
- 1/2 teaspoon ground ginger
- 1/4 teaspoon cayenne pepper (optional, for heat)
- 1 preserved lemon, flesh removed and rind thinly sliced
- 1 cup green olives, pitted
- 1 cup cherry tomatoes, halved
- 1/4 cup fresh cilantro, chopped
- 1/4 cup fresh parsley, chopped
- 2 tablespoons olive oil
- Salt and pepper to taste

Instructions:

1. Preheat your oven to 375°F (190°C).
2. In a large tagine or oven-safe skillet, heat the olive oil over medium heat. Add the chopped onion and minced garlic, and sauté until they become translucent and fragrant.
3. In a small bowl, mix together the ground cumin, coriander, paprika, turmeric, ginger, cayenne pepper (if using), salt, and pepper. Sprinkle this spice mixture over the fish fillets, making sure to coat them evenly.
4. Place the seasoned fish fillets on top of the sautéed onions and garlic in the tagine or skillet. Add the preserved lemon slices, green olives, and cherry tomatoes around the fish.
5. Cover the tagine or skillet with its lid or aluminum foil, and transfer it to the preheated oven. Bake for about 30 minutes, or until the fish is cooked through and flakes easily with a fork.
6. Once the fish is cooked, remove the tagine or skillet from the oven. Sprinkle the chopped cilantro and parsley over the fish and garnish with additional preserved lemon slices if desired.
7. Serve the Fish Tagine with Green Olives and Lemon hot, accompanied by couscous or crusty bread. Enjoy!

Nutrition information (per serving):

- Calories: 280
- Fat: 12g
- Carbohydrates: 10g
- Protein: 32g
- Fiber: 3g

- Sodium: 800mg

54. Moroccan Chicken Tagine with Sweet Potatoes and Prunes

Moroccan Chicken Tagine with Sweet Potatoes and Prunes is a flavorful and aromatic dish that combines tender chicken, sweet potatoes, and juicy prunes in a rich and fragrant sauce. This traditional Moroccan dish is slow-cooked to perfection, allowing the flavors to meld together and create a truly satisfying meal. Serve it with couscous or crusty bread for a complete and hearty dinner.
Serving: 4 servings
Preparation time: 15 minutes
Ready time: 1 hour 30 minutes

Ingredients:
- 4 chicken thighs, bone-in and skin-on
- 2 tablespoons olive oil
- 1 onion, finely chopped
- 3 cloves of garlic, minced
- 1 teaspoon ground cumin
- 1 teaspoon ground coriander
- 1 teaspoon ground cinnamon
- 1 teaspoon paprika
- 1/2 teaspoon ground ginger
- 1/2 teaspoon turmeric
- 1/2 teaspoon salt
- 1/4 teaspoon black pepper
- 2 cups sweet potatoes, peeled and cubed
- 1 cup pitted prunes
- 2 cups chicken broth
- 2 tablespoons honey
- Fresh cilantro, chopped (for garnish)

Instructions:
1. In a large tagine or a heavy-bottomed pot, heat the olive oil over medium heat. Add the chicken thighs, skin-side down, and cook until

browned, about 5 minutes. Flip the chicken and brown the other side for an additional 5 minutes. Remove the chicken from the pot and set aside.
2. In the same pot, add the chopped onion and minced garlic. Sauté until the onion becomes translucent and fragrant, about 5 minutes.
3. Add the ground cumin, coriander, cinnamon, paprika, ginger, turmeric, salt, and black pepper to the pot. Stir well to coat the onions and garlic with the spices.
4. Return the chicken thighs to the pot, along with any accumulated juices. Add the sweet potatoes, prunes, chicken broth, and honey. Stir gently to combine all the Ingredients.
5. Bring the mixture to a boil, then reduce the heat to low. Cover the pot and simmer for 1 hour, or until the chicken is tender and the sweet potatoes are cooked through.
6. Once cooked, remove the lid and simmer for an additional 10 minutes to thicken the sauce slightly.
7. Serve the Moroccan Chicken Tagine with Sweet Potatoes and Prunes hot, garnished with fresh cilantro. It pairs perfectly with couscous or crusty bread.

Nutrition information (per serving):
- Calories: 420
- Fat: 18g
- Carbohydrates: 40g
- Protein: 26g
- Fiber: 6g
- Sugar: 20g
- Sodium: 780mg

55. Lamb and Chickpea Tagine with Spinach

Lamb and Chickpea Tagine with Spinach is a flavorful and hearty Moroccan dish that combines tender lamb, nutritious chickpeas, and vibrant spinach. This aromatic tagine is slow-cooked to perfection, allowing the flavors to meld together and create a comforting and satisfying meal. Serve it with couscous or crusty bread for a complete and delicious dining experience.
Serving: 4 servings
Preparation time: 15 minutes

Ready time: 2 hours 30 minutes

Ingredients:
- 1.5 pounds lamb shoulder, cut into chunks
- 1 onion, finely chopped
- 3 cloves of garlic, minced
- 1 teaspoon ground cumin
- 1 teaspoon ground coriander
- 1 teaspoon ground turmeric
- 1 teaspoon paprika
- 1/2 teaspoon ground cinnamon
- 1/4 teaspoon cayenne pepper (optional, for heat)
- 1 can (14 ounces) chickpeas, drained and rinsed
- 1 can (14 ounces) diced tomatoes
- 1 cup chicken or vegetable broth
- 2 cups fresh spinach leaves
- Salt and pepper to taste
- Fresh cilantro, chopped (for garnish)

Instructions:
1. Heat a large, heavy-bottomed pot or tagine over medium-high heat. Add the lamb chunks and cook until browned on all sides. Remove the lamb from the pot and set aside.
2. In the same pot, add the chopped onion and minced garlic. Sauté until the onion becomes translucent and fragrant.
3. Add the ground cumin, coriander, turmeric, paprika, cinnamon, and cayenne pepper (if using) to the pot. Stir well to coat the onions and garlic with the spices.
4. Return the browned lamb to the pot and add the drained chickpeas, diced tomatoes, and chicken or vegetable broth. Stir everything together to combine.
5. Bring the mixture to a boil, then reduce the heat to low. Cover the pot and let it simmer for about 2 hours, or until the lamb is tender and the flavors have melded together.
6. Just before serving, add the fresh spinach leaves to the pot. Stir them in and let them wilt for a few minutes.
7. Season with salt and pepper to taste. Garnish with fresh chopped cilantro.
8. Serve the Lamb and Chickpea Tagine with Spinach hot, alongside couscous or crusty bread.

Nutrition information:
- Calories: 420
- Fat: 18g
- Carbohydrates: 28g
- Protein: 36g
- Fiber: 8g
- Sodium: 680mg

56. Vegetable Tagine with Honey and Pistachios

Vegetable Tagine with Honey and Pistachios is a delicious and nutritious dish that combines the flavors of tender vegetables, sweet honey, and crunchy pistachios. This Moroccan-inspired recipe is not only easy to make but also packed with vitamins and minerals. Whether you're a vegetarian or simply looking for a healthy and flavorful meal, this Vegetable Tagine is sure to satisfy your taste buds.
Serving: 4 servings
Preparation time: 15 minutes
Ready time: 1 hour

Ingredients:
- 2 tablespoons olive oil
- 1 onion, thinly sliced
- 3 cloves of garlic, minced
- 1 teaspoon ground cumin
- 1 teaspoon ground coriander
- 1 teaspoon ground turmeric
- 1 teaspoon ground cinnamon
- 1 teaspoon paprika
- 1 teaspoon salt
- 1/2 teaspoon black pepper
- 2 carrots, peeled and sliced
- 2 zucchinis, sliced
- 1 red bell pepper, sliced
- 1 yellow bell pepper, sliced
- 1 can (14 ounces) diced tomatoes
- 1 cup vegetable broth

- 2 tablespoons honey
- 1/2 cup shelled pistachios, roughly chopped
- Fresh cilantro or parsley, for garnish (optional)

Instructions:

1. Heat the olive oil in a large pot or tagine over medium heat. Add the sliced onion and minced garlic, and sauté until the onion becomes translucent and fragrant.
2. In a small bowl, combine the ground cumin, coriander, turmeric, cinnamon, paprika, salt, and black pepper. Mix well to create a spice blend.
3. Add the spice blend to the pot and stir it into the onion and garlic mixture, allowing the flavors to meld together for about a minute.
4. Add the sliced carrots, zucchinis, red bell pepper, and yellow bell pepper to the pot. Stir well to coat the vegetables with the spice mixture.
5. Pour in the diced tomatoes and vegetable broth. Stir everything together, then cover the pot and let it simmer for about 45 minutes, or until the vegetables are tender.
6. Stir in the honey and chopped pistachios, allowing them to blend into the tagine for a few minutes.
7. Serve the Vegetable Tagine with Honey and Pistachios hot, garnished with fresh cilantro or parsley if desired. It pairs well with couscous or crusty bread.

Nutrition information per Serving: - Calories: 220

- Fat: 10g
- Carbohydrates: 30g
- Fiber: 7g
- Protein: 6g
- Sodium: 650mg

57. Spicy Harissa Chicken and Chickpea Tagine

Spicy Harissa Chicken and Chickpea Tagine is a flavorful and aromatic Moroccan dish that combines tender chicken, hearty chickpeas, and a spicy harissa sauce. This dish is perfect for those who enjoy a bit of heat and love the rich flavors of North African cuisine. Serve it with couscous or warm crusty bread for a complete and satisfying meal.

Serving: 4 servings
Preparation time: 15 minutes
Ready time: 1 hour 15 minutes

Ingredients:
- 4 chicken thighs, bone-in and skin-on
- 1 tablespoon olive oil
- 1 onion, finely chopped
- 3 cloves of garlic, minced
- 2 tablespoons harissa paste
- 1 teaspoon ground cumin
- 1 teaspoon ground coriander
- 1 teaspoon ground paprika
- 1 can (14 ounces) diced tomatoes
- 1 can (14 ounces) chickpeas, drained and rinsed
- 1 cup chicken broth
- Salt and pepper to taste
- Fresh cilantro, chopped (for garnish)

Instructions:
1. Preheat your oven to 350°F (175°C).
2. In a large oven-safe skillet or tagine, heat the olive oil over medium heat. Add the chicken thighs, skin side down, and cook until golden brown, about 5 minutes. Flip the chicken and cook for an additional 3 minutes. Remove the chicken from the skillet and set aside.
3. In the same skillet, add the chopped onion and minced garlic. Sauté until the onion becomes translucent, about 5 minutes.
4. Stir in the harissa paste, ground cumin, ground coriander, and ground paprika. Cook for 1 minute to release the flavors.
5. Add the diced tomatoes, chickpeas, and chicken broth to the skillet. Season with salt and pepper to taste. Stir well to combine all the Ingredients.
6. Return the chicken thighs to the skillet, nestling them into the sauce. Cover the skillet with a lid or aluminum foil.
7. Transfer the skillet to the preheated oven and bake for 1 hour, or until the chicken is cooked through and tender.
8. Remove the skillet from the oven and let it rest for a few minutes. Garnish with fresh cilantro before serving.
9. Serve the Spicy Harissa Chicken and Chickpea Tagine with couscous or warm crusty bread.

Nutrition information:
- Calories: 380
- Fat: 18g
- Carbohydrates: 25g
- Protein: 30g
- Fiber: 6g
- Sodium: 680mg

58. Moroccan Meatball Tagine with Eggplant and Tomato Sauce

Moroccan Meatball Tagine with Eggplant and Tomato Sauce is a flavorful and aromatic dish that combines tender meatballs with a rich and tangy sauce. This traditional Moroccan recipe is packed with spices and served with fluffy couscous or crusty bread for a satisfying meal. The combination of juicy meatballs, tender eggplant, and a tomato-based sauce creates a harmony of flavors that will transport you to the vibrant streets of Morocco.
Serving: 4 servings
Preparation time: 20 minutes
Ready time: 1 hour 30 minutes

Ingredients:
- 1 lb ground beef or lamb
- 1 small onion, finely chopped
- 2 cloves of garlic, minced
- 1 teaspoon ground cumin
- 1 teaspoon ground coriander
- 1 teaspoon paprika
- 1/2 teaspoon ground cinnamon
- 1/2 teaspoon ground ginger
- 1/4 teaspoon cayenne pepper (optional, for heat)
- Salt and pepper to taste
- 1 egg, beaten
- 1/4 cup breadcrumbs
- 2 tablespoons olive oil
- 1 large eggplant, cut into 1-inch cubes

- 1 can (14 oz) diced tomatoes
- 1 cup vegetable or chicken broth
- 1 tablespoon tomato paste
- Fresh cilantro or parsley, chopped (for garnish)

Instructions:
1. In a large bowl, combine the ground beef or lamb, chopped onion, minced garlic, cumin, coriander, paprika, cinnamon, ginger, cayenne pepper (if using), salt, and pepper. Mix well until all the Ingredients are evenly incorporated.
2. Add the beaten egg and breadcrumbs to the meat mixture. Mix again until everything is well combined. Shape the mixture into small meatballs, about 1 inch in diameter.
3. Heat the olive oil in a large, deep skillet or tagine over medium heat. Add the meatballs and cook until browned on all sides, about 5 minutes. Remove the meatballs from the skillet and set aside.
4. In the same skillet, add the cubed eggplant and cook for 5 minutes, or until slightly softened. Add the diced tomatoes, vegetable or chicken broth, and tomato paste. Stir well to combine.
5. Return the meatballs to the skillet, nestling them into the sauce. Cover the skillet and simmer for 1 hour, or until the meatballs are cooked through and the sauce has thickened.
6. Serve the Moroccan Meatball Tagine with Eggplant and Tomato Sauce over fluffy couscous or with crusty bread. Garnish with fresh cilantro or parsley for added freshness.

Nutrition information:
- Calories: 380
- Fat: 22g
- Carbohydrates: 18g
- Protein: 28g
- Fiber: 5g
- Sugar: 8g
- Sodium: 600mg

59. Chicken and Artichoke Tagine

Chicken and Artichoke Tagine is a delicious and flavorful Moroccan dish that combines tender chicken, tangy artichokes, and aromatic spices. This dish is perfect for a cozy dinner or for entertaining guests. The slow cooking process allows the flavors to meld together, resulting in a mouthwatering meal that will leave everyone wanting more.
Serving: 4 servings
Preparation time: 15 minutes
Ready time: 1 hour 30 minutes

Ingredients:
- 4 chicken thighs, bone-in and skin-on
- 1 tablespoon olive oil
- 1 onion, thinly sliced
- 3 cloves of garlic, minced
- 1 teaspoon ground cumin
- 1 teaspoon ground coriander
- 1 teaspoon ground paprika
- 1/2 teaspoon ground turmeric
- 1/2 teaspoon ground cinnamon
- 1/4 teaspoon cayenne pepper (optional, for heat)
- 1 cup chicken broth
- 1 cup canned artichoke hearts, drained and quartered
- 1 lemon, sliced
- Salt and pepper to taste
- Fresh cilantro or parsley, chopped (for garnish)

Instructions:
1. Season the chicken thighs with salt and pepper. Heat the olive oil in a large tagine or a heavy-bottomed pot over medium-high heat. Add the chicken thighs, skin-side down, and cook until browned, about 5 minutes. Flip the chicken and brown the other side for an additional 5 minutes. Remove the chicken from the pot and set aside.
2. In the same pot, add the sliced onion and minced garlic. Sauté until the onion becomes translucent and fragrant, about 5 minutes.
3. Add the ground cumin, coriander, paprika, turmeric, cinnamon, and cayenne pepper (if using) to the pot. Stir well to coat the onions and garlic with the spices. Cook for an additional 1-2 minutes to toast the spices and release their flavors.

4. Pour in the chicken broth and scrape the bottom of the pot to release any browned bits. Return the chicken thighs to the pot, along with any accumulated juices. Add the artichoke hearts and lemon slices.
5. Reduce the heat to low, cover the pot, and simmer for 1 hour, or until the chicken is tender and cooked through. If using a tagine, make sure to follow the manufacturer's instructions for cooking times and heat settings.
6. Once the chicken is cooked, remove the lid and simmer for an additional 10 minutes to thicken the sauce slightly. Taste and adjust the seasoning with salt and pepper if needed.
7. Serve the Chicken and Artichoke Tagine hot, garnished with fresh cilantro or parsley. This dish pairs well with couscous or crusty bread.

Nutrition information (per serving):
- Calories: 350
- Fat: 18g
- Carbohydrates: 15g
- Protein: 30g
- Fiber: 5g
- Sugar: 3g
- Sodium: 600mg

60. Vegetable and Cauliflower Tagine

Vegetable and Cauliflower Tagine is a delicious and healthy dish that combines the flavors of various vegetables and aromatic spices. This Moroccan-inspired recipe is perfect for those looking for a vegetarian or vegan option that is both satisfying and full of flavor. The tagine is traditionally cooked in a clay pot, but you can easily make it in a regular pot or a slow cooker. With its vibrant colors and fragrant aroma, this Vegetable and Cauliflower Tagine is sure to become a favorite in your household.
Serving: 4 servings
Preparation time: 15 minutes
Ready time: 1 hour 15 minutes

Ingredients:
- 1 cauliflower, cut into florets

- 2 carrots, peeled and sliced
- 1 onion, finely chopped
- 2 garlic cloves, minced
- 1 red bell pepper, sliced
- 1 yellow bell pepper, sliced
- 1 zucchini, sliced
- 1 can (400g) diced tomatoes
- 1 cup vegetable broth
- 1 tablespoon olive oil
- 2 teaspoons ground cumin
- 2 teaspoons ground coriander
- 1 teaspoon ground turmeric
- 1 teaspoon ground cinnamon
- 1 teaspoon paprika
- Salt and pepper to taste
- Fresh cilantro or parsley, chopped (for garnish)

Instructions:
1. Heat the olive oil in a large pot or a tagine over medium heat. Add the chopped onion and minced garlic, and sauté until they become translucent and fragrant.
2. Add the cauliflower florets, sliced carrots, bell peppers, and zucchini to the pot. Stir well to combine.
3. In a small bowl, mix together the ground cumin, coriander, turmeric, cinnamon, paprika, salt, and pepper. Sprinkle this spice mixture over the vegetables in the pot, and stir to coat them evenly.
4. Pour in the diced tomatoes and vegetable broth. Stir everything together, then cover the pot and let it simmer for about 1 hour, or until the vegetables are tender.
5. Once the tagine is cooked, taste and adjust the seasoning if needed.
6. Serve the Vegetable and Cauliflower Tagine hot, garnished with fresh cilantro or parsley. It can be enjoyed on its own or served with couscous or crusty bread.

Nutrition information per Serving: - Calories: 180
- Fat: 4g
- Carbohydrates: 32g
- Fiber: 10g
- Protein: 7g
- Sodium: 480mg

61. Fish Tagine with Saffron and Fennel

Fish Tagine with Saffron and Fennel is a delicious and aromatic Moroccan dish that combines the delicate flavors of fish with the warm spices of saffron and fennel. This dish is perfect for a special occasion or a cozy dinner at home. The slow-cooked tagine method ensures that the fish is tender and infused with all the wonderful flavors of the spices and vegetables.

Serving: 4 servings

Preparation time: 15 minutes

Ready time: 1 hour 30 minutes

Ingredients:

- 1 lb white fish fillets (such as cod or halibut), cut into chunks
- 1 large onion, thinly sliced
- 2 garlic cloves, minced
- 1 fennel bulb, thinly sliced
- 1 red bell pepper, thinly sliced
- 1 can (14 oz) diced tomatoes
- 1 teaspoon ground cumin
- 1 teaspoon ground coriander
- 1/2 teaspoon ground turmeric
- 1/2 teaspoon saffron threads
- 1/4 teaspoon ground cinnamon
- 1/4 teaspoon cayenne pepper (optional, for heat)
- 1/4 cup chopped fresh cilantro
- 2 tablespoons olive oil
- Salt and pepper to taste

Instructions:

1. In a large tagine or a deep skillet with a lid, heat the olive oil over medium heat. Add the sliced onion and cook until softened, about 5 minutes.
2. Add the minced garlic, fennel, and red bell pepper to the tagine. Cook for another 5 minutes, stirring occasionally.

3. In a small bowl, combine the ground cumin, coriander, turmeric, saffron threads, cinnamon, cayenne pepper (if using), salt, and pepper. Mix well.
4. Sprinkle the spice mixture over the vegetables in the tagine and stir to coat evenly.
5. Add the diced tomatoes (with their juice) to the tagine and stir well. Bring the mixture to a simmer.
6. Gently place the fish chunks on top of the vegetable mixture in the tagine. Cover with the lid and let it simmer over low heat for about 1 hour, or until the fish is cooked through and tender.
7. Sprinkle the chopped cilantro over the fish tagine just before serving.
8. Serve the Fish Tagine with Saffron and Fennel hot with couscous or crusty bread.

Nutrition information per Serving: - Calories: 250
- Fat: 10g
- Carbohydrates: 12g
- Protein: 28g
- Fiber: 4g
- Sodium: 400mg

62. Moroccan Chicken Tagine with Apricots and Raisins

Moroccan Chicken Tagine with Apricots and Raisins is a delightful and aromatic dish that combines the flavors of tender chicken, sweet apricots, and plump raisins. This traditional Moroccan recipe is cooked in a tagine, a clay pot with a conical lid that helps to infuse the dish with rich flavors. The combination of spices and dried fruits creates a perfect balance of sweet and savory, making it a favorite among both kids and adults. Serve this delicious tagine with couscous or warm crusty bread for a complete and satisfying meal.
Serving: 4 servings
Preparation time: 15 minutes
Ready time: 1 hour 30 minutes

Ingredients:
- 4 chicken thighs, bone-in and skin-on

- 1 tablespoon olive oil
- 1 onion, finely chopped
- 3 cloves of garlic, minced
- 1 teaspoon ground cumin
- 1 teaspoon ground coriander
- 1 teaspoon ground cinnamon
- 1 teaspoon ground ginger
- 1/2 teaspoon ground turmeric
- 1/2 teaspoon paprika
- 1/4 teaspoon cayenne pepper (optional, for heat)
- 1 cup chicken broth
- 1/2 cup dried apricots, halved
- 1/4 cup raisins
- 2 tablespoons honey
- Salt and pepper, to taste
- Fresh cilantro or parsley, for garnish

Instructions:

1. Heat the olive oil in a tagine or a large, deep skillet over medium heat. Add the chicken thighs, skin side down, and cook until browned and crispy, about 5 minutes. Flip the chicken and cook for an additional 3 minutes. Remove the chicken from the tagine and set aside.
2. In the same tagine, add the chopped onion and minced garlic. Sauté until the onion becomes translucent and fragrant, about 5 minutes.
3. Add the ground cumin, coriander, cinnamon, ginger, turmeric, paprika, and cayenne pepper (if using) to the tagine. Stir well to coat the onions and garlic with the spices. Cook for an additional 2 minutes to toast the spices and release their flavors.
4. Pour in the chicken broth, dried apricots, and raisins. Stir in the honey and season with salt and pepper to taste. Return the chicken thighs to the tagine, nestling them into the sauce.
5. Cover the tagine with its lid and reduce the heat to low. Simmer for 1 hour, or until the chicken is tender and cooked through. Stir occasionally to ensure the chicken is evenly coated with the sauce.
6. Once the chicken is cooked, remove the tagine from the heat. Garnish with fresh cilantro or parsley before serving.

Nutrition information:

- Calories: 380
- Fat: 16g

- Carbohydrates: 32g
- Protein: 28g
- Fiber: 4g
- Sugar: 24g
- Sodium: 480mg

Note: Nutrition information may vary depending on the specific Ingredients and brands used.

63. Lamb and Potato Tagine

Lamb and Potato Tagine is a flavorful and aromatic Moroccan dish that combines tender lamb, potatoes, and a blend of spices. This slow-cooked stew is perfect for a cozy dinner on a chilly evening. The rich flavors and tender meat make it a crowd-pleasing dish that will transport you to the vibrant streets of Morocco.

Serving: 4 servings
Preparation time: 20 minutes
Ready time: 2 hours 30 minutes

Ingredients:
- 1.5 pounds lamb shoulder, cut into chunks
- 2 tablespoons olive oil
- 1 onion, finely chopped
- 3 garlic cloves, minced
- 2 teaspoons ground cumin
- 2 teaspoons ground coriander
- 1 teaspoon ground turmeric
- 1 teaspoon ground cinnamon
- 1 teaspoon paprika
- 1 teaspoon salt
- 1/2 teaspoon black pepper
- 1/4 teaspoon cayenne pepper (optional, for heat)
- 2 cups chicken or vegetable broth
- 1 can (14 ounces) diced tomatoes
- 2 large potatoes, peeled and cut into chunks
- 1/2 cup pitted green olives
- 1/4 cup chopped fresh cilantro, for garnish

Instructions:

1. Heat the olive oil in a large, heavy-bottomed pot or tagine over medium heat. Add the lamb chunks and brown them on all sides. Remove the lamb from the pot and set aside.
2. In the same pot, add the chopped onion and minced garlic. Sauté until the onion becomes translucent and fragrant.
3. Add the ground cumin, coriander, turmeric, cinnamon, paprika, salt, black pepper, and cayenne pepper (if using). Stir well to coat the onions and garlic with the spices.
4. Return the browned lamb to the pot and pour in the chicken or vegetable broth. Stir in the diced tomatoes, including the juice.
5. Bring the mixture to a boil, then reduce the heat to low. Cover the pot and let it simmer for 1 hour, stirring occasionally.
6. After 1 hour, add the potato chunks and green olives to the pot. Stir well to combine. Cover the pot again and continue simmering for another 1 hour, or until the lamb is tender and the potatoes are cooked through.
7. Once the lamb and potatoes are tender, taste the tagine and adjust the seasoning if needed.
8. Serve the Lamb and Potato Tagine hot, garnished with chopped fresh cilantro. It pairs well with couscous or crusty bread.

Nutrition information:

- Calories: 420
- Fat: 18g
- Carbohydrates: 32g
- Protein: 32g
- Fiber: 6g
- Sodium: 980mg

64. Vegetable Tagine with Ginger and Turmeric

Vegetable Tagine with Ginger and Turmeric is a flavorful and aromatic Moroccan dish that is packed with nutritious vegetables and warm spices. This vegetarian tagine is not only delicious but also easy to prepare, making it a perfect choice for a healthy weeknight dinner.

Serving: 4 servings

Preparation time: 15 minutes

Ready time: 1 hour

Ingredients:
- 2 tablespoons olive oil
- 1 onion, diced
- 3 cloves of garlic, minced
- 1 tablespoon fresh ginger, grated
- 1 teaspoon ground turmeric
- 1 teaspoon ground cumin
- 1 teaspoon ground coriander
- 1 teaspoon paprika
- 1 teaspoon cinnamon
- 1 teaspoon salt
- 1/2 teaspoon black pepper
- 2 carrots, peeled and sliced
- 2 zucchinis, sliced
- 1 red bell pepper, sliced
- 1 yellow bell pepper, sliced
- 1 can (14 oz) diced tomatoes
- 1 cup vegetable broth
- 1 cup chickpeas, cooked or canned
- 1/4 cup raisins
- Fresh cilantro, chopped (for garnish)

Instructions:
1. Heat the olive oil in a large pot or tagine over medium heat. Add the diced onion and sauté until translucent, about 5 minutes.
2. Add the minced garlic and grated ginger to the pot and cook for another minute until fragrant.
3. Stir in the ground turmeric, cumin, coriander, paprika, cinnamon, salt, and black pepper. Cook for a minute to toast the spices and release their flavors.
4. Add the sliced carrots, zucchinis, red bell pepper, and yellow bell pepper to the pot. Stir well to coat the vegetables with the spice mixture.
5. Pour in the diced tomatoes and vegetable broth. Bring the mixture to a simmer, then reduce the heat to low and cover the pot. Let it cook for about 45 minutes, or until the vegetables are tender.
6. Stir in the chickpeas and raisins, and cook for an additional 5 minutes to heat them through.
7. Taste and adjust the seasoning if needed.

8. Serve the Vegetable Tagine with Ginger and Turmeric over cooked couscous or rice. Garnish with fresh chopped cilantro.

Nutrition information per Serving: - Calories: 220
- Fat: 7g
- Carbohydrates: 35g
- Fiber: 9g
- Protein: 8g
- Sodium: 800mg

65. Spicy Harissa Shrimp and Vegetable Tagine

Spicy Harissa Shrimp and Vegetable Tagine is a flavorful and aromatic dish inspired by Moroccan cuisine. This dish combines succulent shrimp, vibrant vegetables, and a spicy harissa sauce to create a satisfying and healthy meal. The tagine is traditionally cooked in a clay pot, but can also be prepared in a regular pot or skillet. With its bold flavors and vibrant colors, this dish is sure to impress your family and friends.
Serving: 4 servings
Preparation time: 15 minutes
Ready time: 40 minutes

Ingredients:
- 1 pound large shrimp, peeled and deveined
- 2 tablespoons olive oil
- 1 onion, thinly sliced
- 2 cloves garlic, minced
- 1 red bell pepper, thinly sliced
- 1 yellow bell pepper, thinly sliced
- 1 zucchini, sliced into half-moons
- 1 cup cherry tomatoes, halved
- 2 tablespoons harissa paste
- 1 teaspoon ground cumin
- 1 teaspoon ground coriander
- 1 teaspoon paprika
- 1 teaspoon salt
- 1/2 teaspoon black pepper
- 1 cup vegetable broth

- Fresh cilantro, chopped (for garnish)

Instructions:
1. In a large skillet or tagine pot, heat the olive oil over medium heat. Add the onion and garlic, and sauté until the onion becomes translucent, about 3 minutes.
2. Add the bell peppers, zucchini, and cherry tomatoes to the skillet. Cook for another 5 minutes, stirring occasionally, until the vegetables start to soften.
3. In a small bowl, mix together the harissa paste, cumin, coriander, paprika, salt, and black pepper. Add this spice mixture to the skillet and stir well to coat the vegetables.
4. Add the shrimp to the skillet and cook for 2-3 minutes on each side, until they turn pink and opaque.
5. Pour the vegetable broth into the skillet and bring to a simmer. Reduce the heat to low, cover the skillet, and let it cook for another 10-15 minutes, allowing the flavors to meld together.
6. Remove the lid and garnish with fresh cilantro before serving.

Nutrition information:
- Calories: 250
- Fat: 10g
- Carbohydrates: 12g
- Protein: 25g
- Fiber: 3g
- Sodium: 800mg

Note: Nutrition information may vary depending on the specific Ingredients and brands used.

66. Moroccan Meatball Tagine with Chickpeas

Moroccan Meatball Tagine with Chickpeas is a flavorful and aromatic dish that combines tender meatballs with hearty chickpeas in a rich tomato-based sauce. This traditional Moroccan recipe is packed with spices and herbs, creating a delicious and satisfying meal that will transport you to the vibrant streets of Morocco. Serve it with couscous or crusty bread for a complete and comforting dinner.
Serving: 4 servings

Preparation time: 20 minutes
Ready time: 1 hour 30 minutes

Ingredients:
- 500g ground beef or lamb
- 1 onion, finely chopped
- 3 cloves of garlic, minced
- 1 teaspoon ground cumin
- 1 teaspoon ground coriander
- 1 teaspoon paprika
- 1/2 teaspoon ground cinnamon
- 1/2 teaspoon ground ginger
- 1/4 teaspoon cayenne pepper (optional, for heat)
- Salt and pepper to taste
- 2 tablespoons olive oil
- 1 can (400g) diced tomatoes
- 1 can (400g) chickpeas, drained and rinsed
- 1 cup beef or vegetable broth
- 1 tablespoon tomato paste
- Fresh cilantro or parsley, chopped (for garnish)

Instructions:
1. In a large bowl, combine the ground beef or lamb, chopped onion, minced garlic, ground cumin, ground coriander, paprika, ground cinnamon, ground ginger, cayenne pepper (if using), salt, and pepper. Mix well until all the Ingredients are evenly incorporated.
2. Shape the meat mixture into small meatballs, about 1 inch in diameter.
3. Heat the olive oil in a large tagine or a deep, wide skillet over medium heat. Add the meatballs and cook until browned on all sides, about 5 minutes. Remove the meatballs from the tagine and set aside.
4. In the same tagine or skillet, add the diced tomatoes, chickpeas, beef or vegetable broth, and tomato paste. Stir well to combine.
5. Return the meatballs to the tagine, nestling them into the sauce. Cover the tagine and simmer over low heat for 1 hour, or until the meatballs are cooked through and tender.
6. Serve the Moroccan Meatball Tagine with Chickpeas hot, garnished with fresh cilantro or parsley. It pairs perfectly with couscous or crusty bread.

Nutrition information per Serving: - Calories: 380

- Fat: 20g
- Carbohydrates: 22g
- Protein: 28g
- Fiber: 6g
- Sugar: 5g
- Sodium: 600mg

67. Chicken and Lemon Tagine

Chicken and Lemon Tagine is a delicious Moroccan dish that combines tender chicken with the tangy flavor of lemons and a blend of aromatic spices. This dish is traditionally cooked in a tagine, a clay pot with a conical lid, which helps to infuse the flavors and keep the chicken moist. However, if you don't have a tagine, you can easily make this dish in a regular pot or Dutch oven. Serve this flavorful chicken and lemon tagine with couscous or crusty bread for a complete and satisfying meal.
Serving: 4 servings
Preparation time: 15 minutes
Ready time: 1 hour 30 minutes

Ingredients:
- 4 chicken thighs, bone-in and skin-on
- 2 tablespoons olive oil
- 1 onion, finely chopped
- 3 cloves of garlic, minced
- 1 teaspoon ground cumin
- 1 teaspoon ground coriander
- 1 teaspoon ground turmeric
- 1 teaspoon ground paprika
- 1 preserved lemon, flesh removed and rind thinly sliced
- 1 cup chicken broth
- 1 tablespoon honey
- Salt and pepper to taste
- Fresh cilantro, chopped (for garnish)

Instructions:
1. Heat the olive oil in a tagine or a large pot over medium heat. Add the chicken thighs, skin side down, and cook until browned, about 5

minutes. Flip the chicken and brown the other side for an additional 5 minutes. Remove the chicken from the pot and set aside.
2. In the same pot, add the chopped onion and minced garlic. Sauté until the onion becomes translucent and the garlic is fragrant, about 3 minutes.
3. Add the ground cumin, coriander, turmeric, and paprika to the pot. Stir well to coat the onions and garlic with the spices.
4. Return the chicken thighs to the pot, along with the preserved lemon slices. Pour in the chicken broth and honey. Season with salt and pepper to taste.
5. Cover the pot with a lid and simmer over low heat for 1 hour, or until the chicken is tender and cooked through. If using a tagine, make sure to follow the manufacturer's instructions for cooking times.
6. Once the chicken is cooked, remove it from the pot and set aside. Increase the heat to medium-high and simmer the sauce for an additional 5 minutes, or until it thickens slightly.
7. Return the chicken to the pot and coat it with the sauce. Cook for another 5 minutes to allow the flavors to meld together.
8. Serve the Chicken and Lemon Tagine hot, garnished with fresh cilantro. It pairs well with couscous or crusty bread.

Nutrition information per Serving: - Calories: 350
- Fat: 20g
- Carbohydrates: 10g
- Protein: 30g
- Fiber: 2g

68. Vegetable and Chickpea Tagine with Couscous

Vegetable and Chickpea Tagine with Couscous is a delicious and nutritious dish that combines the flavors of North African cuisine. This vegetarian tagine is packed with a variety of vegetables, protein-rich chickpeas, and aromatic spices. Served over fluffy couscous, it makes for a satisfying and wholesome meal.
Serving: 4 servings
Preparation time: 15 minutes
Ready time: 1 hour

Ingredients:
- 2 tablespoons olive oil
- 1 onion, diced
- 3 cloves of garlic, minced
- 1 teaspoon ground cumin
- 1 teaspoon ground coriander
- 1 teaspoon ground turmeric
- 1 teaspoon paprika
- 1 teaspoon cinnamon
- 1 teaspoon salt
- 1/2 teaspoon black pepper
- 1 can (14 ounces) diced tomatoes
- 1 can (14 ounces) chickpeas, drained and rinsed
- 2 carrots, peeled and sliced
- 1 zucchini, sliced
- 1 red bell pepper, sliced
- 1 cup vegetable broth
- 1 cup couscous
- Fresh cilantro or parsley, for garnish (optional)

Instructions:
1. Heat the olive oil in a large pot or tagine over medium heat. Add the diced onion and minced garlic, and sauté until the onion becomes translucent.
2. Add the ground cumin, coriander, turmeric, paprika, cinnamon, salt, and black pepper to the pot. Stir well to coat the onions and garlic with the spices.
3. Pour in the diced tomatoes, chickpeas, carrots, zucchini, and red bell pepper. Stir to combine all the Ingredients.
4. Pour in the vegetable broth and bring the mixture to a simmer. Reduce the heat to low, cover the pot, and let it cook for about 45 minutes, or until the vegetables are tender.
5. While the tagine is simmering, prepare the couscous according to the package instructions. Fluff it with a fork once cooked.
6. Serve the vegetable and chickpea tagine over a bed of couscous. Garnish with fresh cilantro or parsley, if desired.

Nutrition information per Serving: - Calories: 320
- Fat: 8g
- Carbohydrates: 54g

- Fiber: 10g
- Protein: 11g
- Sodium: 800mg

69. Fish Tagine with Moroccan Spices

Fish Tagine with Moroccan Spices is a flavorful and aromatic dish that combines the delicate flavors of fish with a blend of traditional Moroccan spices. This dish is not only delicious but also easy to prepare, making it a perfect choice for a weeknight dinner or a special occasion. The combination of spices, herbs, and tender fish creates a mouthwatering dish that will transport you to the vibrant streets of Morocco.
Serving: 4 servings
Preparation time: 15 minutes
Ready time: 45 minutes

Ingredients:
- 4 fish fillets (such as cod, halibut, or sea bass)
- 2 tablespoons olive oil
- 1 onion, finely chopped
- 3 garlic cloves, minced
- 1 teaspoon ground cumin
- 1 teaspoon ground coriander
- 1 teaspoon ground paprika
- 1/2 teaspoon ground turmeric
- 1/2 teaspoon ground cinnamon
- 1/4 teaspoon cayenne pepper (optional, for heat)
- 1 cup canned diced tomatoes
- 1 cup vegetable or fish broth
- 1 preserved lemon, sliced (optional)
- 1/4 cup green olives, pitted and halved
- Salt and pepper, to taste
- Fresh cilantro or parsley, chopped (for garnish)

Instructions:

1. In a large tagine or a deep skillet, heat the olive oil over medium heat. Add the chopped onion and minced garlic, and sauté until they become translucent and fragrant.
2. In a small bowl, combine the ground cumin, coriander, paprika, turmeric, cinnamon, and cayenne pepper. Mix well to create a spice blend.
3. Add the spice blend to the skillet and stir it into the onion and garlic mixture. Cook for a minute or two to release the flavors of the spices.
4. Place the fish fillets on top of the onion and spice mixture in the skillet. Pour the diced tomatoes and broth over the fish. Add the preserved lemon slices and green olives.
5. Season with salt and pepper to taste. Cover the skillet with a lid or a tagine top and let it simmer over low heat for about 30 minutes, or until the fish is cooked through and flakes easily with a fork.
6. Once the fish is cooked, remove the skillet from the heat. Garnish with fresh cilantro or parsley.
7. Serve the Fish Tagine with Moroccan Spices hot, accompanied by couscous or crusty bread to soak up the flavorful sauce.

Nutrition information (per serving):
- Calories: 250
- Fat: 10g
- Carbohydrates: 10g
- Protein: 30g
- Fiber: 3g
- Sodium: 600mg

70. Moroccan Chicken Tagine with Green Beans and Tomatoes

Moroccan Chicken Tagine with Green Beans and Tomatoes is a flavorful and aromatic dish that combines tender chicken, crisp green beans, and juicy tomatoes. This traditional Moroccan recipe is cooked in a tagine, a clay pot with a conical lid, which helps to infuse the dish with rich flavors. The combination of spices and herbs creates a deliciously fragrant sauce that pairs perfectly with the tender chicken and vegetables. This dish is not only delicious but also packed with nutrients, making it a wholesome and satisfying meal.

Serving: 4 servings
Preparation time: 15 minutes
Ready time: 1 hour 15 minutes

Ingredients:
- 4 chicken thighs, bone-in and skin-on
- 1 tablespoon olive oil
- 1 onion, finely chopped
- 3 cloves of garlic, minced
- 1 teaspoon ground cumin
- 1 teaspoon ground coriander
- 1 teaspoon ground paprika
- 1 teaspoon ground turmeric
- 1 teaspoon ground cinnamon
- 1 teaspoon salt
- 1/2 teaspoon black pepper
- 1 cup green beans, trimmed and halved
- 2 tomatoes, diced
- 1 cup chicken broth
- 1 tablespoon fresh cilantro, chopped (for garnish)

Instructions:
1. Heat the olive oil in a tagine or a large, deep skillet over medium heat.
2. Add the chicken thighs, skin-side down, and cook for about 5 minutes until browned. Flip the chicken and cook for an additional 5 minutes. Remove the chicken from the tagine and set aside.
3. In the same tagine, add the chopped onion and minced garlic. Sauté for 2-3 minutes until the onion becomes translucent.
4. Add the ground cumin, coriander, paprika, turmeric, cinnamon, salt, and black pepper to the tagine. Stir well to coat the onions and garlic with the spices.
5. Add the green beans and diced tomatoes to the tagine. Stir to combine with the spices.
6. Place the chicken thighs back into the tagine, nestling them into the vegetable mixture.
7. Pour the chicken broth over the chicken and vegetables. Cover the tagine with its lid and simmer over low heat for 1 hour, or until the chicken is cooked through and tender.
8. Once cooked, remove the tagine from the heat and let it rest for a few minutes.

9. Garnish with fresh cilantro before serving.

Nutrition information per Serving: - Calories: 320
- Fat: 18g
- Carbohydrates: 12g
- Protein: 28g
- Fiber: 4g
- Sugar: 5g
- Sodium: 800mg

Note: Nutrition information may vary depending on the specific Ingredients and brands used.

71. Lamb and Carrot Tagine

Lamb and Carrot Tagine is a delicious and aromatic Moroccan dish that combines tender lamb with sweet carrots and a blend of warm spices. This slow-cooked stew is perfect for a cozy dinner on a chilly evening. The flavors of the tender lamb and the fragrant spices will transport you to the vibrant streets of Morocco.
Serving: 4 servings
Preparation time: 20 minutes
Ready time: 2 hours 30 minutes

Ingredients:
- 1.5 pounds lamb shoulder, cut into chunks
- 2 tablespoons olive oil
- 1 onion, finely chopped
- 3 garlic cloves, minced
- 2 teaspoons ground cumin
- 1 teaspoon ground coriander
- 1 teaspoon ground cinnamon
- 1 teaspoon ground ginger
- 1/2 teaspoon ground turmeric
- 1/2 teaspoon paprika
- 1/4 teaspoon cayenne pepper (optional, for heat)
- 4 carrots, peeled and cut into thick slices
- 1 cup chicken or vegetable broth
- 1 tablespoon honey

- 1 tablespoon lemon juice
- Salt and pepper, to taste
- Fresh cilantro or parsley, for garnish

Instructions:

1. Heat the olive oil in a large, heavy-bottomed pot or tagine over medium heat. Add the lamb chunks and brown them on all sides. Remove the lamb from the pot and set aside.
2. In the same pot, add the chopped onion and minced garlic. Sauté until the onion becomes translucent and fragrant.
3. Add the ground cumin, coriander, cinnamon, ginger, turmeric, paprika, and cayenne pepper (if using) to the pot. Stir well to coat the onions and garlic with the spices.
4. Return the browned lamb to the pot and mix it with the onion and spice mixture.
5. Add the sliced carrots, chicken or vegetable broth, honey, and lemon juice to the pot. Season with salt and pepper to taste.
6. Bring the mixture to a boil, then reduce the heat to low. Cover the pot and let the tagine simmer for about 2 hours, or until the lamb is tender and the flavors have melded together.
7. Once the tagine is ready, taste and adjust the seasoning if needed. Garnish with fresh cilantro or parsley before serving.
8. Serve the Lamb and Carrot Tagine hot with couscous or crusty bread.

Nutrition information:

- Calories: 380
- Fat: 18g
- Carbohydrates: 20g
- Protein: 34g
- Fiber: 4g
- Sodium: 450mg

Note: Nutrition information may vary depending on the specific Ingredients and quantities used.

72. Vegetable Tagine with Ras el Hanout and Chickpeas

Vegetable Tagine with Ras el Hanout and Chickpeas is a flavorful and aromatic Moroccan dish that is packed with nutritious vegetables and spices. This vegetarian tagine is not only delicious but also easy to prepare, making it a perfect option for a healthy weeknight dinner.
Serving: 4 servings
Preparation time: 15 minutes
Ready time: 1 hour

Ingredients:
- 2 tablespoons olive oil
- 1 onion, diced
- 3 cloves of garlic, minced
- 2 carrots, peeled and sliced
- 1 red bell pepper, diced
- 1 zucchini, sliced
- 1 eggplant, diced
- 1 can (400g) chickpeas, drained and rinsed
- 2 tablespoons Ras el Hanout spice blend
- 1 can (400g) diced tomatoes
- 1 cup vegetable broth
- Salt and pepper to taste
- Fresh cilantro or parsley, chopped (for garnish)

Instructions:
1. Heat the olive oil in a large pot or tagine over medium heat. Add the diced onion and minced garlic, and sauté until they become translucent and fragrant.
2. Add the sliced carrots, diced red bell pepper, sliced zucchini, and diced eggplant to the pot. Stir well to combine the vegetables.
3. Sprinkle the Ras el Hanout spice blend over the vegetables and mix until they are evenly coated with the spices.
4. Pour in the diced tomatoes and vegetable broth. Stir everything together and season with salt and pepper to taste.
5. Bring the mixture to a boil, then reduce the heat to low. Cover the pot or tagine and let it simmer for about 45 minutes, or until the vegetables are tender.
6. Add the drained and rinsed chickpeas to the pot and stir gently to incorporate them into the tagine. Cook for an additional 5 minutes to heat the chickpeas through.

7. Remove the tagine from the heat and let it rest for a few minutes before serving.
8. Garnish with freshly chopped cilantro or parsley before serving.

Nutrition information (per serving):
- Calories: 250
- Fat: 8g
- Carbohydrates: 38g
- Fiber: 10g
- Protein: 9g
- Sodium: 480mg

73. Spicy Harissa Beef and Vegetable Tagine

Spicy Harissa Beef and Vegetable Tagine is a flavorful and aromatic Moroccan dish that combines tender beef, a medley of vegetables, and a spicy harissa sauce. This dish is perfect for those who enjoy a bit of heat and love exploring new flavors. The slow cooking process allows the flavors to meld together, resulting in a delicious and satisfying meal.
Serving: 4 servings
Preparation time: 20 minutes
Ready time: 2 hours 30 minutes

Ingredients:
- 1.5 pounds beef stew meat, cut into cubes
- 2 tablespoons olive oil
- 1 onion, diced
- 3 cloves garlic, minced
- 2 carrots, peeled and sliced
- 2 bell peppers, diced
- 1 zucchini, sliced
- 1 can (14 ounces) diced tomatoes
- 2 tablespoons harissa paste
- 1 teaspoon ground cumin
- 1 teaspoon ground coriander
- 1 teaspoon paprika
- 1 teaspoon salt
- 1/2 teaspoon black pepper

- 2 cups beef broth
- Fresh cilantro, chopped (for garnish)

Instructions:
1. Heat the olive oil in a large pot or tagine over medium heat. Add the beef cubes and brown them on all sides. Remove the beef from the pot and set aside.
2. In the same pot, add the diced onion and minced garlic. Sauté until the onion becomes translucent and fragrant.
3. Add the carrots, bell peppers, and zucchini to the pot. Cook for about 5 minutes, until the vegetables start to soften.
4. Return the beef to the pot and add the diced tomatoes, harissa paste, cumin, coriander, paprika, salt, and black pepper. Stir well to combine all the Ingredients.
5. Pour in the beef broth and bring the mixture to a boil. Once boiling, reduce the heat to low and cover the pot. Let the tagine simmer for about 2 hours, or until the beef is tender and the flavors have melded together.
6. Serve the Spicy Harissa Beef and Vegetable Tagine hot, garnished with fresh cilantro. It pairs well with couscous or crusty bread.

Nutrition information (per serving):
- Calories: 380
- Fat: 18g
- Carbohydrates: 20g
- Protein: 34g
- Fiber: 5g
- Sugar: 9g
- Sodium: 950mg

74. Moroccan Meatball Tagine with Zucchini

Moroccan Meatball Tagine with Zucchini is a flavorful and aromatic dish that combines tender meatballs with zucchini in a rich tomato-based sauce. This traditional Moroccan recipe is packed with spices and herbs, creating a delicious and satisfying meal that will transport you to the vibrant streets of Morocco. Serve it with couscous or crusty bread for a complete and hearty dinner.

Serving: 4 servings
Preparation time: 20 minutes
Ready time: 1 hour

Ingredients:
- 500g ground beef or lamb
- 1 small onion, finely chopped
- 2 cloves of garlic, minced
- 1 teaspoon ground cumin
- 1 teaspoon ground coriander
- 1 teaspoon paprika
- 1/2 teaspoon ground cinnamon
- 1/2 teaspoon ground ginger
- 1/4 teaspoon cayenne pepper (optional, for heat)
- Salt and pepper to taste
- 2 tablespoons olive oil
- 1 can (400g) diced tomatoes
- 2 zucchinis, sliced into rounds
- 1 cup beef or vegetable broth
- Fresh cilantro or parsley, chopped (for garnish)

Instructions:
1. In a large bowl, combine the ground meat, chopped onion, minced garlic, cumin, coriander, paprika, cinnamon, ginger, cayenne pepper (if using), salt, and pepper. Mix well until all the Ingredients are evenly incorporated.
2. Shape the meat mixture into small meatballs, about 1 inch in diameter.
3. Heat the olive oil in a large tagine or a deep skillet over medium heat. Add the meatballs and cook until browned on all sides, about 5 minutes. Remove the meatballs from the tagine and set aside.
4. In the same tagine, add the diced tomatoes and zucchini slices. Stir in the beef or vegetable broth and season with salt and pepper to taste.
5. Return the meatballs to the tagine, nestling them among the zucchini and tomatoes. Cover the tagine and simmer over low heat for 45 minutes to 1 hour, or until the meatballs are cooked through and the zucchini is tender.
6. Serve the Moroccan Meatball Tagine with Zucchini hot, garnished with fresh cilantro or parsley. It pairs perfectly with couscous or crusty bread.

Nutrition information per Serving: - Calories: 350
- Fat: 20g
- Carbohydrates: 10g
- Protein: 30g
- Fiber: 3g

75. Chicken and Olive Tagine with Preserved Lemons

Chicken and Olive Tagine with Preserved Lemons is a flavorful and aromatic Moroccan dish that combines tender chicken, briny olives, and tangy preserved lemons. This traditional tagine is slow-cooked to perfection, allowing the flavors to meld together and create a truly delicious meal. Serve it with couscous or crusty bread for a complete and satisfying dinner.
Serving: 4 servings
Preparation time: 15 minutes
Ready time: 1 hour 30 minutes

Ingredients:
- 4 chicken thighs, bone-in and skin-on
- 1 onion, finely chopped
- 3 cloves of garlic, minced
- 1 teaspoon ground cumin
- 1 teaspoon ground coriander
- 1 teaspoon ground paprika
- 1/2 teaspoon ground turmeric
- 1/4 teaspoon ground cinnamon
- 1/4 teaspoon ground ginger
- 1/4 teaspoon cayenne pepper (optional, for heat)
- 1 cup green olives, pitted
- 2 preserved lemons, flesh removed and rind thinly sliced
- 1 cup chicken broth
- 2 tablespoons olive oil
- Salt and pepper to taste
- Fresh cilantro or parsley, chopped (for garnish)

Instructions:

1. In a large tagine or a heavy-bottomed pot, heat the olive oil over medium heat. Add the chicken thighs, skin-side down, and cook until browned and crispy, about 5 minutes. Flip the chicken and brown the other side for an additional 5 minutes. Remove the chicken from the pot and set aside.
2. In the same pot, add the chopped onion and minced garlic. Sauté until the onion becomes translucent and fragrant, about 5 minutes.
3. Add the ground cumin, coriander, paprika, turmeric, cinnamon, ginger, and cayenne pepper (if using) to the pot. Stir well to coat the onions and garlic with the spices. Cook for an additional 2 minutes to toast the spices and release their flavors.
4. Return the chicken thighs to the pot, along with any accumulated juices. Add the green olives and preserved lemon slices. Pour in the chicken broth, ensuring that the chicken is partially submerged. Season with salt and pepper to taste.
5. Cover the pot and reduce the heat to low. Allow the tagine to simmer gently for 1 hour, or until the chicken is tender and cooked through. Stir occasionally to prevent sticking and to distribute the flavors.
6. Once the chicken is cooked, remove the tagine from the heat. Garnish with fresh cilantro or parsley.
7. Serve the Chicken and Olive Tagine with Preserved Lemons hot, accompanied by couscous or crusty bread.

Nutrition information (per serving):
- Calories: 380
- Fat: 22g
- Carbohydrates: 10g
- Protein: 35g
- Fiber: 3g
- Sugar: 2g
- Sodium: 900mg

76. Vegetable and Sweet Potato Tagine

Vegetable and Sweet Potato Tagine is a delicious and hearty Moroccan-inspired dish that is packed with flavor and nutrients. This vegetarian tagine is made with a combination of vegetables, sweet potatoes, and

aromatic spices, creating a comforting and satisfying meal. It is perfect for a cozy dinner or for entertaining guests.
Serving: 4 servings
Preparation time: 15 minutes
Ready time: 1 hour

Ingredients:
- 2 tablespoons olive oil
- 1 onion, diced
- 3 cloves of garlic, minced
- 2 teaspoons ground cumin
- 1 teaspoon ground coriander
- 1 teaspoon ground turmeric
- 1 teaspoon ground cinnamon
- 1 teaspoon paprika
- 1/2 teaspoon ground ginger
- 1/4 teaspoon cayenne pepper (optional, for heat)
- 2 sweet potatoes, peeled and cut into chunks
- 2 carrots, peeled and sliced
- 1 red bell pepper, sliced
- 1 zucchini, sliced
- 1 can (14 oz) diced tomatoes
- 1 cup vegetable broth
- 1 cup chickpeas, drained and rinsed
- Salt and pepper to taste
- Fresh cilantro or parsley, chopped (for garnish)

Instructions:
1. Heat the olive oil in a large pot or tagine over medium heat. Add the diced onion and minced garlic, and sauté until the onion becomes translucent and fragrant.
2. Add the ground cumin, coriander, turmeric, cinnamon, paprika, ginger, and cayenne pepper (if using) to the pot. Stir well to coat the onions and garlic with the spices, and cook for another minute to release their flavors.
3. Add the sweet potatoes, carrots, red bell pepper, and zucchini to the pot. Stir to combine with the spices.
4. Pour in the diced tomatoes and vegetable broth. Bring the mixture to a simmer, then cover the pot and reduce the heat to low. Let it cook for about 45 minutes, or until the sweet potatoes and vegetables are tender.

5. Stir in the chickpeas and season with salt and pepper to taste. Cook for an additional 5 minutes to heat the chickpeas through.
6. Serve the Vegetable and Sweet Potato Tagine hot, garnished with fresh cilantro or parsley. It can be enjoyed on its own or served with couscous or crusty bread.

Nutrition information per Serving: - Calories: 250
- Fat: 7g
- Carbohydrates: 42g
- Fiber: 9g
- Protein: 7g
- Sodium: 480mg

77. Fish Tagine with Harissa and Tomatoes

Fish Tagine with Harissa and Tomatoes is a flavorful and aromatic dish that combines the delicate flavors of fish with the boldness of harissa and tomatoes. This Moroccan-inspired dish is perfect for seafood lovers who enjoy a bit of spice and tang in their meals. The tagine cooking method ensures that the fish remains tender and moist, while the harissa and tomatoes infuse the dish with a rich and vibrant flavor. Serve this dish with couscous or crusty bread for a complete and satisfying meal.
Serving: 4 servings
Preparation time: 15 minutes
Ready time: 45 minutes

Nutrition information: (per serving)
- Calories: 250
- Fat: 10g
- Carbohydrates: 10g
- Protein: 30g

Ingredients:
- 4 fish fillets (such as cod, halibut, or sea bass)
- 2 tablespoons olive oil
- 1 onion, thinly sliced
- 3 garlic cloves, minced
- 2 tablespoons harissa paste

- 1 teaspoon ground cumin
- 1 teaspoon ground coriander
- 1 teaspoon paprika
- 1 can (400g) diced tomatoes
- 1 cup vegetable or fish broth
- Salt and pepper, to taste
- Fresh cilantro or parsley, for garnish

Instructions:

1. Preheat your oven to 375°F (190°C).
2. In a large oven-safe skillet or tagine, heat the olive oil over medium heat. Add the sliced onion and minced garlic, and sauté until the onion becomes translucent and fragrant.
3. Stir in the harissa paste, ground cumin, ground coriander, and paprika. Cook for an additional 2 minutes to allow the spices to release their flavors.
4. Add the diced tomatoes and broth to the skillet, and season with salt and pepper to taste. Stir well to combine all the Ingredients.
5. Place the fish fillets on top of the tomato mixture, ensuring they are fully submerged in the sauce. Cover the skillet or tagine with a lid or aluminum foil.
6. Transfer the skillet or tagine to the preheated oven and bake for 25-30 minutes, or until the fish is cooked through and flakes easily with a fork.
7. Once cooked, remove the skillet or tagine from the oven and let it rest for a few minutes. Garnish with fresh cilantro or parsley before serving.
8. Serve the Fish Tagine with Harissa and Tomatoes hot, accompanied by couscous or crusty bread.

Note: You can adjust the amount of harissa paste according to your desired level of spiciness. Additionally, feel free to add other vegetables such as bell peppers or zucchini to the tagine for added flavor and texture.

78. Moroccan Chicken Tagine with Potatoes and Peas

Moroccan Chicken Tagine with Potatoes and Peas is a flavorful and aromatic dish that combines tender chicken, hearty potatoes, and vibrant peas in a rich and fragrant sauce. This traditional Moroccan recipe is a

perfect blend of spices and Ingredients that will transport you to the exotic flavors of North Africa. Whether you're hosting a dinner party or simply craving a comforting meal, this tagine is sure to impress.
Serving: 4 servings
Preparation time: 15 minutes
Ready time: 1 hour 15 minutes

Ingredients:
- 4 chicken thighs, bone-in and skin-on
- 2 tablespoons olive oil
- 1 onion, finely chopped
- 3 cloves of garlic, minced
- 1 teaspoon ground cumin
- 1 teaspoon ground coriander
- 1 teaspoon ground paprika
- 1 teaspoon ground turmeric
- 1 teaspoon ground cinnamon
- 1 teaspoon salt
- 1/2 teaspoon black pepper
- 2 potatoes, peeled and cut into chunks
- 1 cup frozen peas
- 1 cup chicken broth
- 1 tablespoon honey
- Fresh cilantro, chopped (for garnish)

Instructions:
1. In a large tagine or a deep, heavy-bottomed skillet, heat the olive oil over medium heat. Add the chicken thighs, skin-side down, and cook until browned and crispy, about 5 minutes. Flip the chicken and cook for an additional 3 minutes. Remove the chicken from the tagine and set aside.
2. In the same tagine, add the chopped onion and minced garlic. Sauté until the onion becomes translucent and fragrant, about 5 minutes.
3. Add the ground cumin, coriander, paprika, turmeric, cinnamon, salt, and black pepper to the tagine. Stir well to coat the onions and garlic with the spices.
4. Return the chicken thighs to the tagine, placing them on top of the onion and spice mixture. Add the potato chunks and frozen peas around the chicken.

5. Pour the chicken broth over the chicken and vegetables. Drizzle the honey over the top.
6. Cover the tagine and simmer over low heat for 1 hour, or until the chicken is cooked through and the potatoes are tender. Stir occasionally to ensure even cooking.
7. Once cooked, remove the tagine from the heat. Garnish with fresh chopped cilantro.

Nutrition information per Serving: - Calories: 380
- Fat: 18g
- Carbohydrates: 25g
- Protein: 30g
- Fiber: 5g
- Sugar: 6g
- Sodium: 800mg

Note: Nutrition information may vary depending on the specific Ingredients and brands used.

79. Lamb and Prune Tagine with Almonds

Lamb and Prune Tagine with Almonds is a delicious Moroccan dish that combines tender lamb, sweet prunes, and crunchy almonds. This slow-cooked stew is bursting with flavors and aromas, making it the perfect comfort food for any occasion. The combination of savory and sweet Ingredients creates a harmonious balance that will leave your taste buds wanting more. Serve this hearty dish with couscous or crusty bread for a complete meal that will transport you to the vibrant streets of Morocco.
Serving: 4 servings
Preparation time: 20 minutes
Ready time: 2 hours 30 minutes

Ingredients:
- 1.5 pounds lamb shoulder, cut into chunks
- 1 onion, finely chopped
- 3 cloves of garlic, minced
- 1 teaspoon ground cumin
- 1 teaspoon ground coriander
- 1 teaspoon ground cinnamon

- 1 teaspoon paprika
- 1/2 teaspoon ground ginger
- 1/4 teaspoon cayenne pepper (optional, for heat)
- 1 cup pitted prunes
- 1/2 cup whole almonds
- 2 tablespoons olive oil
- 2 cups chicken or vegetable broth
- Salt and pepper to taste
- Fresh cilantro or parsley, for garnish

Instructions:
1. In a large tagine or heavy-bottomed pot, heat the olive oil over medium heat. Add the lamb chunks and brown them on all sides. Remove the lamb from the pot and set aside.
2. In the same pot, add the chopped onion and minced garlic. Sauté until the onion becomes translucent and fragrant.
3. Add the ground cumin, coriander, cinnamon, paprika, ginger, and cayenne pepper (if using) to the pot. Stir well to coat the onions and garlic with the spices.
4. Return the browned lamb to the pot and mix it with the onion and spice mixture. Season with salt and pepper to taste.
5. Pour in the chicken or vegetable broth, ensuring that the lamb is fully submerged. Bring the mixture to a boil, then reduce the heat to low and cover the pot. Let it simmer for 2 hours, or until the lamb is tender and easily falls apart.
6. After 2 hours, add the pitted prunes and whole almonds to the pot. Stir gently to combine all the Ingredients. Cover the pot again and let it simmer for an additional 30 minutes, allowing the flavors to meld together.
7. Once the lamb is tender and the prunes have softened, remove the pot from the heat. Let it rest for a few minutes before serving.
8. Serve the Lamb and Prune Tagine with Almonds hot, garnished with fresh cilantro or parsley. Accompany it with couscous or crusty bread for a complete meal.

Nutrition information (per serving):
- Calories: 450
- Fat: 25g
- Carbohydrates: 25g
- Protein: 35g

- Fiber: 5g
- Sugar: 15g
- Sodium: 600mg

80. Vegetable Tagine with Chickpeas and Spinach

Vegetable Tagine with Chickpeas and Spinach is a flavorful and nutritious dish that combines the richness of Moroccan spices with the freshness of vegetables. This vegetarian tagine is not only delicious but also packed with essential nutrients, making it a perfect choice for a healthy and satisfying meal.
Serving: 4 servings
Preparation time: 15 minutes
Ready time: 1 hour

Ingredients:
- 2 tablespoons olive oil
- 1 onion, diced
- 3 cloves of garlic, minced
- 1 teaspoon ground cumin
- 1 teaspoon ground coriander
- 1 teaspoon ground turmeric
- 1 teaspoon paprika
- 1/2 teaspoon ground cinnamon
- 1/4 teaspoon cayenne pepper (optional, for heat)
- 2 carrots, peeled and sliced
- 1 red bell pepper, diced
- 1 zucchini, sliced
- 1 can (14 ounces) chickpeas, drained and rinsed
- 1 can (14 ounces) diced tomatoes
- 1 cup vegetable broth
- 2 cups fresh spinach leaves
- Salt and pepper to taste
- Fresh cilantro or parsley, chopped (for garnish)

Instructions:

1. Heat the olive oil in a large pot or tagine over medium heat. Add the diced onion and minced garlic, and sauté until they become translucent and fragrant.
2. Add the ground cumin, coriander, turmeric, paprika, cinnamon, and cayenne pepper (if using) to the pot. Stir well to coat the onions and garlic with the spices.
3. Add the sliced carrots, diced red bell pepper, and sliced zucchini to the pot. Cook for about 5 minutes, until the vegetables start to soften.
4. Pour in the drained chickpeas, diced tomatoes, and vegetable broth. Stir everything together and bring the mixture to a simmer.
5. Reduce the heat to low, cover the pot, and let the tagine simmer for about 45 minutes to 1 hour, or until the vegetables are tender and the flavors have melded together.
6. Stir in the fresh spinach leaves and cook for an additional 2-3 minutes, until the spinach wilts.
7. Season with salt and pepper to taste.
8. Serve the Vegetable Tagine with Chickpeas and Spinach hot, garnished with fresh cilantro or parsley.

Nutrition information per Serving: - Calories: 250
- Fat: 8g
- Carbohydrates: 38g
- Fiber: 10g
- Protein: 10g
- Sodium: 600mg

81. Spicy Harissa Lamb and Vegetable Tagine

Spicy Harissa Lamb and Vegetable Tagine is a flavorful and aromatic dish that combines tender lamb, a medley of vegetables, and a spicy harissa sauce. This Moroccan-inspired tagine is perfect for those who enjoy a bit of heat and a burst of exotic flavors. It is a hearty and satisfying meal that will transport your taste buds to the vibrant streets of Marrakech.
Serving: 4 servings
Preparation time: 20 minutes
Ready time: 2 hours

Ingredients:
- 1.5 pounds lamb shoulder, cut into chunks
- 2 tablespoons olive oil
- 1 onion, finely chopped
- 3 garlic cloves, minced
- 2 carrots, peeled and sliced
- 1 red bell pepper, sliced
- 1 zucchini, sliced
- 1 can (14 ounces) diced tomatoes
- 2 tablespoons harissa paste
- 1 teaspoon ground cumin
- 1 teaspoon ground coriander
- 1 teaspoon ground cinnamon
- 1 teaspoon paprika
- Salt and pepper to taste
- Fresh cilantro, chopped (for garnish)

Instructions:
1. Heat the olive oil in a large tagine or a heavy-bottomed pot over medium heat. Add the lamb chunks and brown them on all sides. Remove the lamb from the pot and set it aside.
2. In the same pot, add the chopped onion and minced garlic. Sauté until the onion becomes translucent and fragrant.
3. Add the sliced carrots, red bell pepper, and zucchini to the pot. Cook for a few minutes until the vegetables start to soften.
4. Return the browned lamb to the pot and add the diced tomatoes, harissa paste, ground cumin, ground coriander, ground cinnamon, paprika, salt, and pepper. Stir well to combine all the Ingredients.
5. Cover the pot and let the tagine simmer on low heat for about 2 hours, or until the lamb is tender and the flavors have melded together.
6. Once the tagine is ready, taste and adjust the seasoning if needed. Serve the Spicy Harissa Lamb and Vegetable Tagine hot, garnished with fresh cilantro.

Nutrition information:
- Calories: 380
- Fat: 18g
- Carbohydrates: 18g
- Protein: 35g
- Fiber: 5g

- Sodium: 450mg

82. Moroccan Meatball Tagine with Bell Peppers

Moroccan Meatball Tagine with Bell Peppers is a flavorful and aromatic dish that combines tender meatballs with the sweetness of bell peppers and the richness of Moroccan spices. This traditional Moroccan dish is perfect for a hearty and satisfying meal.
Serving: 4 servings
Preparation time: 20 minutes
Ready time: 1 hour 30 minutes

Ingredients:
- 500g ground beef
- 1 onion, finely chopped
- 3 cloves of garlic, minced
- 1 teaspoon ground cumin
- 1 teaspoon ground coriander
- 1 teaspoon paprika
- 1/2 teaspoon ground cinnamon
- 1/2 teaspoon ground ginger
- 1/4 teaspoon cayenne pepper (optional, for heat)
- Salt and pepper to taste
- 2 tablespoons olive oil
- 2 red bell peppers, sliced
- 2 yellow bell peppers, sliced
- 1 can (400g) diced tomatoes
- 1 cup beef or vegetable broth
- Fresh cilantro or parsley, chopped (for garnish)

Instructions:
1. In a large bowl, combine the ground beef, chopped onion, minced garlic, ground cumin, ground coriander, paprika, ground cinnamon, ground ginger, cayenne pepper (if using), salt, and pepper. Mix well until all the Ingredients are evenly incorporated.
2. Shape the meat mixture into small meatballs, about 1 inch in diameter.

3. Heat the olive oil in a large tagine or a deep skillet over medium heat. Add the meatballs and cook until browned on all sides, about 5 minutes. Remove the meatballs from the tagine and set aside.
4. In the same tagine, add the sliced bell peppers and cook for 5 minutes until slightly softened.
5. Return the meatballs to the tagine and add the diced tomatoes and beef or vegetable broth. Stir gently to combine all the Ingredients.
6. Cover the tagine and simmer over low heat for 1 hour, or until the meatballs are cooked through and the flavors have melded together.
7. Serve the Moroccan Meatball Tagine with Bell Peppers hot, garnished with fresh cilantro or parsley. It pairs well with couscous or crusty bread.

Nutrition information per Serving: - Calories: 350
- Fat: 20g
- Carbohydrates: 15g
- Protein: 25g
- Fiber: 4g
- Sugar: 8g
- Sodium: 600mg

83. Chicken and Vegetable Tagine with Saffron Rice

Chicken and Vegetable Tagine with Saffron Rice is a flavorful and aromatic dish inspired by Moroccan cuisine. This dish combines tender chicken, a medley of vegetables, and fragrant spices, all cooked together in a traditional tagine pot. Served with saffron-infused rice, this dish is a perfect balance of flavors and textures that will transport you to the exotic flavors of Morocco.
Serving: 4 servings
Preparation time: 15 minutes
Ready time: 1 hour 30 minutes

Ingredients:
- 4 chicken thighs, bone-in and skin-on
- 1 onion, finely chopped
- 3 cloves of garlic, minced
- 1 red bell pepper, sliced
- 1 zucchini, sliced

- 1 carrot, sliced
- 1 cup cherry tomatoes
- 1 tablespoon olive oil
- 1 teaspoon ground cumin
- 1 teaspoon ground coriander
- 1 teaspoon ground paprika
- 1 teaspoon ground turmeric
- 1 teaspoon ground cinnamon
- 1 teaspoon salt
- 1/2 teaspoon black pepper
- 1 cup chicken broth
- 1/4 cup chopped fresh cilantro
- 1/4 cup chopped fresh parsley

For the saffron rice:
- 1 cup basmati rice
- 2 cups water
- 1/2 teaspoon saffron threads
- 1/2 teaspoon salt

Instructions:
1. In a large tagine pot or a heavy-bottomed pot, heat the olive oil over medium heat. Add the chicken thighs, skin side down, and cook until browned, about 5 minutes. Flip the chicken and cook for an additional 3 minutes. Remove the chicken from the pot and set aside.
2. In the same pot, add the chopped onion and minced garlic. Sauté until the onion becomes translucent, about 5 minutes.
3. Add the sliced bell pepper, zucchini, carrot, and cherry tomatoes to the pot. Stir in the ground cumin, coriander, paprika, turmeric, cinnamon, salt, and black pepper. Cook for 5 minutes, until the vegetables start to soften.
4. Return the chicken thighs to the pot, nestling them among the vegetables. Pour in the chicken broth and bring to a simmer. Cover the pot and cook for 1 hour, or until the chicken is cooked through and tender.
5. While the tagine is cooking, prepare the saffron rice. In a separate pot, bring 2 cups of water to a boil. Add the basmati rice, saffron threads, and salt. Reduce the heat to low, cover the pot, and simmer for 15 minutes, or until the rice is cooked and fluffy.
6. Once the chicken is cooked, remove the tagine pot from the heat. Sprinkle the chopped cilantro and parsley over the tagine.

7. Serve the Chicken and Vegetable Tagine over the saffron rice, garnished with additional fresh herbs if desired.

Nutrition information:
- Calories: 380
- Fat: 15g
- Carbohydrates: 35g
- Protein: 25g
- Fiber: 5g
- Sodium: 800mg

84. Vegetable and Eggplant Tagine with Couscous

Vegetable and Eggplant Tagine with Couscous is a delicious and healthy Moroccan-inspired dish that is packed with flavors and nutrients. This vegetarian recipe combines tender eggplant, a variety of vegetables, and aromatic spices, all cooked together in a flavorful tomato-based sauce. Served over fluffy couscous, this tagine is a satisfying and wholesome meal that will please both vegetarians and meat-lovers alike.
Serving: 4 servings
Preparation time: 15 minutes
Ready time: 45 minutes

Ingredients:
- 2 large eggplants, cut into 1-inch cubes
- 2 tablespoons olive oil
- 1 onion, finely chopped
- 3 cloves of garlic, minced
- 1 red bell pepper, sliced
- 1 yellow bell pepper, sliced
- 2 zucchinis, sliced
- 1 can (14 oz) diced tomatoes
- 1 tablespoon tomato paste
- 1 teaspoon ground cumin
- 1 teaspoon ground coriander
- 1 teaspoon ground paprika
- 1 teaspoon ground turmeric
- 1 teaspoon salt

- 1/2 teaspoon black pepper
- 1/4 teaspoon cayenne pepper (optional, for heat)
- 1 cup vegetable broth
- 1 cup couscous
- Fresh cilantro or parsley, chopped (for garnish)

Instructions:
1. Preheat the oven to 400°F (200°C). Place the eggplant cubes on a baking sheet and drizzle with 1 tablespoon of olive oil. Toss to coat the eggplant evenly. Roast in the oven for about 20 minutes or until the eggplant is tender and slightly browned.
2. In a large pot or tagine, heat the remaining tablespoon of olive oil over medium heat. Add the chopped onion and minced garlic, and sauté until the onion becomes translucent and fragrant.
3. Add the sliced bell peppers and zucchinis to the pot, and cook for about 5 minutes until they start to soften.
4. Stir in the diced tomatoes, tomato paste, ground cumin, ground coriander, ground paprika, ground turmeric, salt, black pepper, and cayenne pepper (if using). Mix well to combine all the flavors.
5. Add the roasted eggplant cubes to the pot, along with the vegetable broth. Stir everything together, cover the pot, and let it simmer for about 20 minutes, allowing the flavors to meld together.
6. While the tagine is simmering, prepare the couscous according to the package instructions. Fluff it with a fork once cooked.
7. To serve, spoon the vegetable and eggplant tagine over a bed of fluffy couscous. Garnish with freshly chopped cilantro or parsley.

Nutrition information per Serving: - Calories: 320
- Fat: 8g
- Carbohydrates: 58g
- Fiber: 12g
- Protein: 9g
- Sodium: 800mg

Note: Nutrition information may vary depending on the specific Ingredients and brands used.

85. Fish Tagine with Tomato and Onion Sauce

Fish Tagine with Tomato and Onion Sauce is a delicious and flavorful dish that combines the delicate taste of fish with a rich and tangy tomato and onion sauce. This Moroccan-inspired recipe is easy to make and perfect for a weeknight dinner or a special occasion. The fish is gently simmered in the sauce, allowing it to absorb all the wonderful flavors. Serve this dish with couscous or crusty bread for a complete and satisfying meal.
Serving: 4 servings
Preparation time: 15 minutes
Ready time: 45 minutes

Ingredients:
- 4 fish fillets (such as cod, halibut, or sea bass)
- 2 tablespoons olive oil
- 1 onion, thinly sliced
- 2 garlic cloves, minced
- 1 red bell pepper, thinly sliced
- 1 can (14 ounces) diced tomatoes
- 1 teaspoon ground cumin
- 1 teaspoon ground paprika
- 1 teaspoon ground turmeric
- 1 teaspoon ground cinnamon
- Salt and pepper to taste
- Fresh cilantro or parsley, chopped (for garnish)

Instructions:
1. Heat the olive oil in a large skillet or tagine over medium heat. Add the sliced onion and cook until softened, about 5 minutes.
2. Add the minced garlic and sliced red bell pepper to the skillet. Cook for another 2 minutes, stirring occasionally.
3. Stir in the diced tomatoes, ground cumin, ground paprika, ground turmeric, and ground cinnamon. Season with salt and pepper to taste.
4. Reduce the heat to low and let the sauce simmer for 10 minutes, allowing the flavors to meld together.
5. Gently place the fish fillets into the sauce, making sure they are submerged. Cover the skillet or tagine and cook for 15-20 minutes, or until the fish is cooked through and flakes easily with a fork.
6. Remove the skillet or tagine from the heat and let it sit for a few minutes before serving.

7. Garnish with fresh cilantro or parsley and serve the Fish Tagine with Tomato and Onion Sauce hot with couscous or crusty bread.

Nutrition information (per serving):
- Calories: 250
- Fat: 10g
- Carbohydrates: 10g
- Protein: 30g
- Fiber: 3g
- Sugar: 5g
- Sodium: 400mg

86. Moroccan Chicken Tagine with Green Olives and Preserved Lemons

Moroccan Chicken Tagine with Green Olives and Preserved Lemons is a flavorful and aromatic dish that combines tender chicken with the tanginess of green olives and the unique taste of preserved lemons. This traditional Moroccan dish is slow-cooked in a tagine, a clay pot with a conical lid, which helps to infuse all the flavors together. The result is a deliciously tender and fragrant chicken dish that will transport you to the vibrant streets of Morocco.
Serving: 4 servings
Preparation time: 15 minutes
Ready time: 1 hour 30 minutes

Ingredients:
- 4 chicken thighs, bone-in and skin-on
- 2 tablespoons olive oil
- 1 onion, finely chopped
- 3 cloves of garlic, minced
- 1 teaspoon ground cumin
- 1 teaspoon ground coriander
- 1 teaspoon ground paprika
- 1 teaspoon ground turmeric
- 1 teaspoon ground ginger
- 1/2 teaspoon ground cinnamon
- 1/2 teaspoon ground black pepper

- 1/2 teaspoon salt
- 1 cup green olives, pitted
- 2 preserved lemons, flesh removed and rind thinly sliced
- 1 cup chicken broth
- Fresh cilantro, chopped (for garnish)

Instructions:

1. Heat the olive oil in a tagine or a large, deep skillet over medium heat.
2. Add the chicken thighs, skin-side down, and cook until browned, about 5 minutes. Flip the chicken and brown the other side for an additional 5 minutes. Remove the chicken from the tagine and set aside.
3. In the same tagine, add the chopped onion and minced garlic. Sauté until the onion becomes translucent and fragrant, about 5 minutes.
4. Add the ground cumin, coriander, paprika, turmeric, ginger, cinnamon, black pepper, and salt to the tagine. Stir well to coat the onions and garlic with the spices.
5. Return the chicken thighs to the tagine, nestling them into the onion and spice mixture.
6. Add the green olives and preserved lemon slices to the tagine, distributing them evenly around the chicken.
7. Pour the chicken broth over the chicken and bring the mixture to a simmer.
8. Cover the tagine with its lid and reduce the heat to low. Let the chicken simmer for 1 hour, or until the meat is tender and cooked through.
9. Once the chicken is cooked, remove the tagine from the heat and let it rest for a few minutes.
10. Garnish with freshly chopped cilantro before serving.
11. Serve the Moroccan Chicken Tagine with Green Olives and Preserved Lemons with couscous or crusty bread to soak up the flavorful sauce.

Nutrition information (per serving):

- Calories: 380
- Fat: 24g
- Carbohydrates: 10g
- Protein: 32g
- Fiber: 3g

87. Lamb and Cauliflower Tagine

Lamb and Cauliflower Tagine is a flavorful and aromatic Moroccan dish that combines tender lamb with cauliflower and a blend of spices. This hearty and comforting dish is perfect for a cozy dinner or a special occasion. The slow cooking process allows the flavors to meld together, resulting in a delicious and tender meal.
Serving: 4 servings
Preparation time: 20 minutes
Ready time: 2 hours 30 minutes

Ingredients:
- 1.5 pounds lamb shoulder, cut into chunks
- 1 large cauliflower, cut into florets
- 1 onion, finely chopped
- 3 cloves of garlic, minced
- 2 tablespoons olive oil
- 1 teaspoon ground cumin
- 1 teaspoon ground coriander
- 1 teaspoon ground turmeric
- 1 teaspoon ground cinnamon
- 1 teaspoon paprika
- 1 teaspoon salt
- 1/2 teaspoon black pepper
- 1 cup chicken broth
- 1/4 cup dried apricots, chopped
- 1/4 cup raisins
- 2 tablespoons honey
- Fresh cilantro, chopped (for garnish)

Instructions:
1. In a large tagine or a heavy-bottomed pot, heat the olive oil over medium heat. Add the lamb chunks and brown them on all sides. Remove the lamb from the pot and set aside.
2. In the same pot, add the chopped onion and minced garlic. Sauté until the onion becomes translucent and fragrant.
3. Add the ground cumin, coriander, turmeric, cinnamon, paprika, salt, and black pepper to the pot. Stir well to coat the onions and garlic with the spices.

4. Return the browned lamb to the pot and mix it with the onion and spice mixture.
5. Add the cauliflower florets, dried apricots, raisins, and chicken broth to the pot. Stir everything together.
6. Cover the pot and simmer on low heat for about 2 hours, or until the lamb is tender and the flavors have melded together.
7. Stir in the honey and cook for an additional 10 minutes to allow the flavors to blend.
8. Serve the Lamb and Cauliflower Tagine hot, garnished with fresh cilantro. It pairs well with couscous or rice.

Nutrition information:
- Calories: 420
- Fat: 18g
- Carbohydrates: 30g
- Protein: 35g
- Fiber: 6g
- Sodium: 780mg

88. Vegetable Tagine with Spicy Harissa Sauce

Vegetable Tagine with Spicy Harissa Sauce is a flavorful and aromatic Moroccan dish that combines a variety of vegetables with a spicy and tangy harissa sauce. This vegetarian dish is not only delicious but also packed with nutrients, making it a perfect choice for a healthy and satisfying meal.
Serving: 4 servings
Preparation time: 15 minutes
Ready time: 1 hour

Ingredients:
- 2 tablespoons olive oil
- 1 onion, diced
- 3 cloves of garlic, minced
- 1 teaspoon ground cumin
- 1 teaspoon ground coriander
- 1 teaspoon ground turmeric
- 1 teaspoon paprika

- 1/2 teaspoon ground cinnamon
- 1/4 teaspoon cayenne pepper (adjust according to your spice preference)
- 1 red bell pepper, sliced
- 1 yellow bell pepper, sliced
- 2 carrots, sliced
- 1 zucchini, sliced
- 1 eggplant, diced
- 1 can (14 oz) diced tomatoes
- 1 cup vegetable broth
- 2 tablespoons harissa paste
- Salt and pepper to taste
- Fresh cilantro or parsley for garnish

Instructions:
1. Heat the olive oil in a large pot or tagine over medium heat. Add the diced onion and minced garlic, and sauté until they become translucent and fragrant.
2. Add the ground cumin, coriander, turmeric, paprika, cinnamon, and cayenne pepper to the pot. Stir well to coat the onions and garlic with the spices.
3. Add the sliced bell peppers, carrots, zucchini, and diced eggplant to the pot. Stir and cook for about 5 minutes, until the vegetables start to soften.
4. Pour in the diced tomatoes and vegetable broth. Stir in the harissa paste and season with salt and pepper to taste.
5. Bring the mixture to a boil, then reduce the heat to low. Cover the pot and let it simmer for about 45 minutes to 1 hour, or until the vegetables are tender and the flavors have melded together.
6. Serve the Vegetable Tagine with Spicy Harissa Sauce hot, garnished with fresh cilantro or parsley. It can be enjoyed on its own or served with couscous or crusty bread.

Nutrition information per Serving: - Calories: 180
- Fat: 8g
- Carbohydrates: 25g
- Fiber: 8g
- Protein: 4g
- Sodium: 480mg

89. Spicy Harissa Chicken and Chickpea Tagine with Couscous

This Spicy Harissa Chicken and Chickpea Tagine with Couscous is a flavorful and aromatic dish that combines tender chicken, hearty chickpeas, and a spicy harissa sauce. The tagine is slow-cooked to perfection, allowing all the flavors to meld together and create a deliciously satisfying meal. Served over fluffy couscous, this dish is sure to impress your family and friends.
Serving: 4 servings
Preparation time: 15 minutes
Ready time: 1 hour 30 minutes

Ingredients:
- 4 chicken thighs, bone-in and skin-on
- 1 tablespoon olive oil
- 1 onion, diced
- 3 cloves of garlic, minced
- 2 tablespoons harissa paste
- 1 teaspoon ground cumin
- 1 teaspoon ground coriander
- 1 teaspoon ground paprika
- 1 can (14 ounces) diced tomatoes
- 1 can (14 ounces) chickpeas, drained and rinsed
- 1 cup chicken broth
- Salt and pepper, to taste
- Fresh cilantro, chopped (for garnish)
- 2 cups cooked couscous

Instructions:
1. Preheat your oven to 350°F (175°C).
2. In a large oven-safe skillet or tagine, heat the olive oil over medium heat. Add the chicken thighs, skin-side down, and cook until browned, about 5 minutes. Flip the chicken and brown the other side for an additional 5 minutes. Remove the chicken from the skillet and set aside.
3. In the same skillet, add the diced onion and minced garlic. Sauté until the onion becomes translucent, about 5 minutes.

4. Stir in the harissa paste, ground cumin, ground coriander, and ground paprika. Cook for another 2 minutes to allow the spices to release their flavors.
5. Add the diced tomatoes, chickpeas, and chicken broth to the skillet. Season with salt and pepper to taste. Stir well to combine all the Ingredients.
6. Return the chicken thighs to the skillet, nestling them into the sauce. Cover the skillet with a lid or foil and transfer it to the preheated oven.
7. Bake for 1 hour, or until the chicken is cooked through and tender.
8. While the tagine is cooking, prepare the couscous according to the package instructions.
9. Once the chicken is done, remove the skillet from the oven. Serve the Spicy Harissa Chicken and Chickpea Tagine over the cooked couscous. Garnish with fresh cilantro.
10. Enjoy!

Nutrition information:
- Calories: 450
- Fat: 18g
- Carbohydrates: 40g
- Protein: 32g
- Fiber: 8g

90. Moroccan Meatball Tagine with Squash and Tomato Sauce

Moroccan Meatball Tagine with Squash and Tomato Sauce is a flavorful and aromatic dish that combines tender meatballs with a rich and tangy tomato sauce. This traditional Moroccan recipe is packed with spices and served with a side of squash, creating a hearty and satisfying meal. Whether you're looking to impress guests or simply want to enjoy a taste of Morocco at home, this dish is sure to delight your taste buds.
Serving: 4 servings
Preparation time: 20 minutes
Ready time: 1 hour 30 minutes

Ingredients:
- 1 pound ground beef

- 1/2 cup breadcrumbs
- 1/4 cup chopped fresh parsley
- 1/4 cup chopped fresh cilantro
- 1 small onion, finely chopped
- 2 cloves garlic, minced
- 1 teaspoon ground cumin
- 1 teaspoon ground coriander
- 1/2 teaspoon ground cinnamon
- 1/2 teaspoon paprika
- 1/4 teaspoon cayenne pepper (optional, for heat)
- Salt and pepper to taste
- 2 tablespoons olive oil
- 1 onion, sliced
- 2 cloves garlic, minced
- 1 can (14 ounces) diced tomatoes
- 1 cup chicken or vegetable broth
- 1 small butternut squash, peeled, seeded, and cut into cubes
- Fresh cilantro, for garnish

Instructions:

1. In a large bowl, combine the ground beef, breadcrumbs, parsley, cilantro, chopped onion, minced garlic, cumin, coriander, cinnamon, paprika, cayenne pepper (if using), salt, and pepper. Mix well until all the Ingredients are evenly incorporated.
2. Shape the mixture into small meatballs, about 1 inch in diameter.
3. Heat the olive oil in a large tagine or a deep skillet over medium heat. Add the sliced onion and minced garlic, and sauté until they become translucent and fragrant.
4. Add the diced tomatoes and broth to the tagine or skillet, and bring the mixture to a simmer.
5. Gently place the meatballs into the sauce, making sure they are evenly distributed. Cover the tagine or skillet and let it simmer for about 45 minutes, or until the meatballs are cooked through.
6. Add the cubed butternut squash to the tagine or skillet, and continue to simmer for an additional 15 minutes, or until the squash is tender.
7. Serve the Moroccan meatball tagine hot, garnished with fresh cilantro. It pairs well with couscous or crusty bread.

Nutrition information:

- Calories: 350 per Serving: - Fat: 18g

- Carbohydrates: 25g
- Protein: 25g
- Fiber: 5g
- Sodium: 600mg

91. Chicken and Apricot Tagine

Chicken and Apricot Tagine is a delicious Moroccan dish that combines tender chicken with the sweetness of apricots and the aromatic flavors of various spices. This hearty and flavorful dish is perfect for a cozy dinner or for entertaining guests. The slow cooking process allows the flavors to meld together, resulting in a dish that is both comforting and exotic.
Serving: 4 servings
Preparation time: 15 minutes
Ready time: 1 hour 30 minutes

Ingredients:
- 4 chicken thighs, bone-in and skin-on
- 1 onion, finely chopped
- 3 cloves of garlic, minced
- 1 teaspoon ground cumin
- 1 teaspoon ground coriander
- 1 teaspoon ground ginger
- 1 teaspoon ground cinnamon
- 1/2 teaspoon ground turmeric
- 1/2 teaspoon paprika
- 1/4 teaspoon cayenne pepper (optional, for heat)
- 1 cup dried apricots
- 1 cup chicken broth
- 2 tablespoons honey
- 2 tablespoons olive oil
- Salt and pepper to taste
- Fresh cilantro or parsley, chopped (for garnish)

Instructions:
1. In a large tagine or a heavy-bottomed pot, heat the olive oil over medium heat. Add the chicken thighs, skin-side down, and cook until

browned, about 5 minutes. Flip the chicken and brown the other side for an additional 5 minutes. Remove the chicken from the pot and set aside.
2. In the same pot, add the chopped onion and minced garlic. Sauté until the onion becomes translucent and fragrant, about 5 minutes.
3. Add the ground cumin, coriander, ginger, cinnamon, turmeric, paprika, and cayenne pepper (if using) to the pot. Stir well to coat the onions and garlic with the spices. Cook for an additional 2 minutes to toast the spices and release their flavors.
4. Return the chicken thighs to the pot, along with any accumulated juices. Add the dried apricots, chicken broth, and honey. Season with salt and pepper to taste.
5. Bring the mixture to a simmer, then reduce the heat to low. Cover the pot and let it cook for 1 hour, or until the chicken is tender and cooked through. Stir occasionally to prevent sticking.
6. Once the chicken is cooked, remove it from the pot and set aside. Increase the heat to medium-high and let the sauce reduce for about 5 minutes, or until it thickens slightly.
7. Serve the chicken and apricot tagine over cooked couscous or rice. Garnish with fresh cilantro or parsley.

Nutrition information per Serving: - Calories: 380
- Fat: 16g
- Carbohydrates: 32g
- Protein: 28g
- Fiber: 4g
- Sugar: 24g
- Sodium: 450mg

Note: Nutrition information may vary depending on the specific Ingredients and brands used.

92. Vegetable and Lentil Tagine with Turmeric Rice

This Vegetable and Lentil Tagine with Turmeric Rice is a delicious and nutritious dish that combines the flavors of Moroccan cuisine with the goodness of vegetables and lentils. The tagine is packed with aromatic spices and tender vegetables, while the turmeric rice adds a vibrant color and earthy flavor. This recipe is perfect for a hearty and satisfying meal that is both vegetarian and gluten-free.

Serving: 4 servings
Preparation time: 15 minutes
Ready time: 1 hour

Ingredients:
For the Vegetable and Lentil Tagine:
- 1 tablespoon olive oil
- 1 onion, diced
- 3 cloves of garlic, minced
- 1 teaspoon ground cumin
- 1 teaspoon ground coriander
- 1 teaspoon ground turmeric
- 1 teaspoon ground paprika
- 1 teaspoon ground cinnamon
- 1 cup dried lentils, rinsed and drained
- 2 carrots, peeled and sliced
- 2 zucchinis, sliced
- 1 red bell pepper, diced
- 1 can (14 oz) diced tomatoes
- 2 cups vegetable broth
- Salt and pepper to taste
- Fresh cilantro, chopped (for garnish)

For the Turmeric Rice:
- 1 cup basmati rice
- 2 cups water
- 1 teaspoon ground turmeric
- Salt to taste

Instructions:
1. Heat the olive oil in a large pot or tagine over medium heat. Add the diced onion and minced garlic, and sauté until they become translucent and fragrant.
2. Add the ground cumin, coriander, turmeric, paprika, and cinnamon to the pot. Stir well to coat the onions and garlic with the spices.
3. Add the rinsed lentils, sliced carrots, zucchinis, and diced red bell pepper to the pot. Stir to combine all the Ingredients.
4. Pour in the diced tomatoes and vegetable broth. Season with salt and pepper to taste. Bring the mixture to a boil, then reduce the heat to low and cover the pot. Let it simmer for about 45 minutes, or until the lentils and vegetables are tender.

5. While the tagine is simmering, prepare the turmeric rice. In a separate pot, combine the basmati rice, water, ground turmeric, and salt. Bring to a boil, then reduce the heat to low and cover the pot. Let it cook for about 15-20 minutes, or until the rice is fluffy and cooked through.
6. Once the tagine and rice are ready, serve the vegetable and lentil tagine over a bed of turmeric rice. Garnish with fresh chopped cilantro.

Nutrition information per Serving: - Calories: 320
- Fat: 4g
- Carbohydrates: 60g
- Fiber: 12g
- Protein: 14g
- Sodium: 600mg
Note: Nutrition information may vary depending on the specific Ingredients and brands used.

93. Fish Tagine with Cilantro and Lime

Fish Tagine with Cilantro and Lime is a delicious and aromatic Moroccan dish that combines the flavors of fresh fish, fragrant spices, and zesty lime. This dish is perfect for seafood lovers and those who enjoy a burst of citrusy flavors in their meals. The tagine cooking method ensures that the fish remains tender and moist, while the cilantro and lime add a refreshing twist to the dish. Serve this Fish Tagine with Cilantro and Lime with couscous or crusty bread for a complete and satisfying meal.
Serving: 4 servings
Preparation time: 15 minutes
Ready time: 45 minutes

Ingredients:
- 4 fish fillets (such as cod, halibut, or sea bass)
- 2 tablespoons olive oil
- 1 onion, finely chopped
- 3 garlic cloves, minced
- 1 teaspoon ground cumin
- 1 teaspoon ground coriander
- 1 teaspoon paprika
- 1 teaspoon ground turmeric

- 1 teaspoon salt
- 1/2 teaspoon black pepper
- 1 cup canned diced tomatoes
- 1/4 cup chopped fresh cilantro
- Juice and zest of 1 lime
- Lime wedges, for Serving:

Instructions:

1. Preheat the oven to 375°F (190°C).
2. In a large oven-safe skillet or tagine, heat the olive oil over medium heat. Add the chopped onion and minced garlic, and sauté until the onion becomes translucent and the garlic is fragrant.
3. In a small bowl, combine the ground cumin, coriander, paprika, turmeric, salt, and black pepper. Mix well.
4. Sprinkle the spice mixture over the onion and garlic in the skillet, and stir to coat evenly.
5. Add the canned diced tomatoes to the skillet, and stir to combine with the spices.
6. Place the fish fillets on top of the tomato mixture in the skillet. Spoon some of the tomato mixture over the fish.
7. Cover the skillet with a lid or foil, and transfer it to the preheated oven. Bake for 25-30 minutes, or until the fish is cooked through and flakes easily with a fork.
8. Remove the skillet from the oven, and sprinkle the chopped cilantro, lime juice, and lime zest over the fish.
9. Serve the Fish Tagine with Cilantro and Lime hot, with lime wedges on the side for an extra burst of citrus flavor.

Nutrition information:

- Calories: 250
- Fat: 10g
- Carbohydrates: 8g
- Protein: 30g
- Fiber: 2g

94. Moroccan Chicken Tagine with Carrots and Green Beans

Moroccan Chicken Tagine with Carrots and Green Beans is a flavorful and aromatic dish that combines tender chicken with a medley of vegetables and traditional Moroccan spices. This dish is slow-cooked in a tagine, a traditional Moroccan clay pot, which helps to infuse all the flavors together. The result is a delicious and hearty meal that is perfect for any occasion.
Serving: 4 servings
Preparation time: 15 minutes
Ready time: 1 hour 30 minutes

Ingredients:
- 4 chicken thighs, bone-in and skin-on
- 2 tablespoons olive oil
- 1 onion, finely chopped
- 3 cloves of garlic, minced
- 2 teaspoons ground cumin
- 2 teaspoons ground coriander
- 1 teaspoon ground turmeric
- 1 teaspoon ground cinnamon
- 1 teaspoon paprika
- 1 teaspoon salt
- 1/2 teaspoon black pepper
- 1 cup chicken broth
- 1 cup diced tomatoes
- 1 cup sliced carrots
- 1 cup green beans, trimmed
- 1/4 cup chopped fresh cilantro, for garnish

Instructions:
1. Heat the olive oil in a tagine or a large, deep skillet over medium heat. Add the chicken thighs, skin-side down, and cook until browned, about 5 minutes. Flip the chicken and brown the other side for an additional 5 minutes. Remove the chicken from the tagine and set aside.
2. In the same tagine, add the chopped onion and minced garlic. Sauté until the onion becomes translucent, about 5 minutes.
3. Add the ground cumin, ground coriander, ground turmeric, ground cinnamon, paprika, salt, and black pepper to the tagine. Stir well to coat the onions and garlic with the spices.
4. Pour in the chicken broth and diced tomatoes. Stir to combine everything together.

5. Return the chicken thighs to the tagine, nestling them into the sauce. Cover the tagine and simmer over low heat for 1 hour, or until the chicken is cooked through and tender.
6. Add the sliced carrots and green beans to the tagine. Cover and continue to simmer for an additional 15 minutes, or until the vegetables are tender.
7. Remove the tagine from the heat and let it rest for a few minutes. Garnish with chopped fresh cilantro before serving.

Nutrition information:
- Calories: 320
- Fat: 18g
- Carbohydrates: 12g
- Protein: 28g
- Fiber: 4g
- Sugar: 5g
- Sodium: 800mg
Note: Nutrition information may vary depending on the specific Ingredients and brands used.

95. Lamb and Spinach Tagine

Lamb and Spinach Tagine is a flavorful and aromatic Moroccan dish that combines tender lamb with nutritious spinach and a blend of spices. This hearty and comforting dish is perfect for a cozy dinner or a special occasion. The slow cooking process allows the flavors to meld together, resulting in a delicious and satisfying meal.
Serving: 4 servings
Preparation time: 20 minutes
Ready time: 2 hours 30 minutes

Ingredients:
- 1.5 pounds lamb shoulder, cut into chunks
- 1 onion, finely chopped
- 3 cloves of garlic, minced
- 2 tablespoons olive oil
- 1 teaspoon ground cumin
- 1 teaspoon ground coriander

- 1 teaspoon ground turmeric
- 1 teaspoon ground cinnamon
- 1/2 teaspoon ground ginger
- 1/2 teaspoon paprika
- 1/4 teaspoon cayenne pepper (optional, for heat)
- Salt and pepper to taste
- 1 cup chicken or vegetable broth
- 1 can diced tomatoes (14 ounces)
- 2 cups fresh spinach leaves
- 1/4 cup chopped fresh cilantro (optional, for garnish)
- Lemon wedges, for Serving:

Instructions:

1. In a large tagine or a heavy-bottomed pot, heat the olive oil over medium heat. Add the chopped onion and minced garlic, and sauté until they become translucent and fragrant.
2. Add the lamb chunks to the pot and brown them on all sides. This will help seal in the juices and add flavor to the dish.
3. In a small bowl, combine the ground cumin, coriander, turmeric, cinnamon, ginger, paprika, cayenne pepper (if using), salt, and pepper. Mix well to create a spice blend.
4. Sprinkle the spice blend over the browned lamb, stirring well to coat the meat evenly. Allow the spices to toast for a minute or two, releasing their aromas.
5. Pour in the chicken or vegetable broth and diced tomatoes, including their juices. Stir everything together, scraping the bottom of the pot to release any browned bits.
6. Reduce the heat to low, cover the pot, and let the tagine simmer for about 2 hours, or until the lamb becomes tender and starts to fall apart.
7. Stir in the fresh spinach leaves and cook for an additional 5 minutes, or until the spinach wilts and becomes tender.
8. Taste and adjust the seasoning if needed. If you prefer a thicker sauce, you can simmer the tagine uncovered for a few more minutes to reduce the liquid.
9. Serve the Lamb and Spinach Tagine hot, garnished with chopped fresh cilantro (if desired) and accompanied by lemon wedges for squeezing over the dish. This tagine pairs well with couscous or crusty bread.

Nutrition information:

- Calories: 380

- Fat: 22g
- Carbohydrates: 12g
- Protein: 34g
- Fiber: 3g
- Sodium: 600mg

Note: Nutrition information may vary depending on the specific Ingredients and brands used.

96. Vegetable Tagine with Chickpeas and Almonds

Vegetable Tagine with Chickpeas and Almonds is a delicious and nutritious dish that combines the flavors of North African cuisine. This vegetarian tagine is packed with a variety of vegetables, protein-rich chickpeas, and crunchy almonds. It is a perfect dish for those looking for a healthy and flavorful meal.

Serving: 4 servings

Preparation time: 15 minutes

Ready time: 1 hour

Ingredients:

- 2 tablespoons olive oil
- 1 onion, diced
- 3 cloves of garlic, minced
- 1 teaspoon ground cumin
- 1 teaspoon ground coriander
- 1 teaspoon ground turmeric
- 1 teaspoon paprika
- 1/2 teaspoon ground cinnamon
- 1/4 teaspoon cayenne pepper (optional, for heat)
- 1 red bell pepper, diced
- 1 yellow bell pepper, diced
- 2 carrots, peeled and sliced
- 1 zucchini, sliced
- 1 eggplant, diced
- 1 can (15 ounces) chickpeas, drained and rinsed
- 1 can (14 ounces) diced tomatoes
- 1 cup vegetable broth
- 1/2 cup sliced almonds

- Salt and pepper to taste
- Fresh cilantro or parsley for garnish

Instructions:
1. Heat the olive oil in a large pot or tagine over medium heat. Add the diced onion and minced garlic, and sauté until the onion becomes translucent.
2. Add the ground cumin, coriander, turmeric, paprika, cinnamon, and cayenne pepper (if using) to the pot. Stir well to coat the onions and garlic with the spices.
3. Add the diced red and yellow bell peppers, sliced carrots, zucchini, and diced eggplant to the pot. Stir to combine the vegetables with the spices.
4. Pour in the drained and rinsed chickpeas, diced tomatoes, and vegetable broth. Stir everything together and bring the mixture to a simmer.
5. Reduce the heat to low, cover the pot, and let the tagine simmer for about 45 minutes to 1 hour, or until the vegetables are tender.
6. While the tagine is simmering, toast the sliced almonds in a dry skillet over medium heat until they become golden and fragrant. Set aside.
7. Once the vegetables are cooked, season the tagine with salt and pepper to taste. Serve the vegetable tagine hot, garnished with toasted almonds and fresh cilantro or parsley.

Nutrition information per Serving: - Calories: 320
- Fat: 14g
- Carbohydrates: 42g
- Fiber: 12g
- Protein: 11g
- Sodium: 480mg

97. Spicy Harissa Vegetable and Quinoa Tagine

This Spicy Harissa Vegetable and Quinoa Tagine is a flavorful and nutritious dish that combines the bold flavors of harissa with a medley of vegetables and quinoa. It is a perfect option for those looking for a healthy and satisfying meal that is also vegan and gluten-free. The combination of spices and vegetables creates a deliciously spicy and aromatic tagine that will leave you wanting more.

Serving: 4 servings
Preparation time: 15 minutes
Ready time: 45 minutes

Ingredients:

- 1 tablespoon olive oil
- 1 onion, diced
- 3 cloves of garlic, minced
- 2 carrots, peeled and sliced
- 1 red bell pepper, diced
- 1 zucchini, diced
- 1 cup cooked chickpeas
- 1 cup quinoa, rinsed
- 2 cups vegetable broth
- 2 tablespoons harissa paste
- 1 teaspoon ground cumin
- 1 teaspoon ground coriander
- 1 teaspoon paprika
- Salt and pepper to taste
- Fresh cilantro, chopped (for garnish)

Instructions:

1. Heat the olive oil in a large pot or tagine over medium heat. Add the diced onion and minced garlic, and sauté until the onion becomes translucent.
2. Add the sliced carrots, diced red bell pepper, and diced zucchini to the pot. Cook for about 5 minutes, until the vegetables start to soften.
3. Stir in the cooked chickpeas, rinsed quinoa, vegetable broth, harissa paste, ground cumin, ground coriander, paprika, salt, and pepper. Bring the mixture to a boil.
4. Reduce the heat to low, cover the pot, and let it simmer for about 30 minutes, or until the quinoa is cooked and the vegetables are tender.
5. Once cooked, remove the pot from the heat and let it sit for a few minutes before serving.
6. Garnish with fresh chopped cilantro and serve hot.

Nutrition information:

- Calories: 320
- Fat: 7g
- Carbohydrates: 55g

- Fiber: 10g
- Protein: 12g
- Sodium: 480mg

98. Moroccan Meatball Tagine with Peppers and Tomato Sauce

Moroccan Meatball Tagine with Peppers and Tomato Sauce is a flavorful and aromatic dish that combines tender meatballs with a rich tomato sauce and the vibrant flavors of Moroccan spices. This dish is perfect for a cozy family dinner or for entertaining guests. The combination of juicy meatballs, sweet peppers, and tangy tomato sauce will surely delight your taste buds.
Serving: 4 servings
Preparation time: 20 minutes
Ready time: 1 hour 10 minutes

Ingredients:
- 500g ground beef
- 1 onion, finely chopped
- 3 cloves of garlic, minced
- 1 teaspoon ground cumin
- 1 teaspoon ground coriander
- 1 teaspoon paprika
- 1/2 teaspoon ground cinnamon
- 1/2 teaspoon ground ginger
- 1/4 teaspoon cayenne pepper (optional, for heat)
- Salt and pepper to taste
- 2 tablespoons olive oil
- 2 red bell peppers, sliced
- 2 yellow bell peppers, sliced
- 1 can (400g) diced tomatoes
- 1 tablespoon tomato paste
- 1 cup beef or vegetable broth
- Fresh cilantro or parsley, chopped (for garnish)

Instructions:

1. In a large bowl, combine the ground beef, chopped onion, minced garlic, ground cumin, ground coriander, paprika, ground cinnamon, ground ginger, cayenne pepper (if using), salt, and pepper. Mix well until all the Ingredients are evenly incorporated.
2. Shape the meat mixture into small meatballs, about 1 inch in diameter.
3. Heat the olive oil in a large tagine or a deep skillet over medium heat. Add the meatballs and cook until browned on all sides, about 5 minutes. Remove the meatballs from the tagine and set aside.
4. In the same tagine, add the sliced bell peppers and cook for 5 minutes until slightly softened.
5. Add the diced tomatoes, tomato paste, and beef or vegetable broth to the tagine. Stir well to combine.
6. Return the meatballs to the tagine, nestling them into the tomato sauce and peppers. Cover the tagine and simmer for 45 minutes to 1 hour, until the meatballs are cooked through and the flavors have melded together.
7. Serve the Moroccan Meatball Tagine with Peppers and Tomato Sauce hot, garnished with fresh cilantro or parsley. This dish pairs well with couscous or crusty bread.

Nutrition information:
- Calories: 350 per Serving: - Fat: 20g
- Carbohydrates: 15g
- Protein: 25g
- Fiber: 4g
- Sugar: 8g
- Sodium: 600mg

99. Chicken and Date Tagine

Chicken and Date Tagine is a delicious Moroccan dish that combines tender chicken with sweet dates and aromatic spices. This hearty and flavorful dish is perfect for a cozy dinner or a special occasion. The slow cooking process allows the flavors to meld together, resulting in a dish that is both comforting and exotic.
Serving: 4 servings
Preparation time: 15 minutes
Ready time: 1 hour 30 minutes

Ingredients:
- 4 chicken thighs, bone-in and skin-on
- 1 tablespoon olive oil
- 1 onion, finely chopped
- 3 cloves of garlic, minced
- 1 teaspoon ground cumin
- 1 teaspoon ground coriander
- 1 teaspoon ground cinnamon
- 1 teaspoon ground ginger
- 1/2 teaspoon ground turmeric
- 1/2 teaspoon paprika
- 1 cup pitted dates
- 1 cup chicken broth
- 1 tablespoon honey
- Salt and pepper to taste
- Fresh cilantro, chopped (for garnish)

Instructions:
1. Heat the olive oil in a large tagine or a heavy-bottomed pot over medium heat.
2. Season the chicken thighs with salt and pepper, then add them to the pot, skin side down. Cook until the skin is golden brown and crispy, about 5 minutes. Flip the chicken and cook for an additional 3 minutes. Remove the chicken from the pot and set aside.
3. In the same pot, add the chopped onion and minced garlic. Sauté until the onion is translucent and fragrant, about 5 minutes.
4. Add the ground cumin, coriander, cinnamon, ginger, turmeric, and paprika to the pot. Stir well to coat the onions and garlic with the spices.
5. Return the chicken thighs to the pot, along with any juices that may have accumulated. Add the pitted dates, chicken broth, and honey. Stir to combine.
6. Reduce the heat to low, cover the pot, and simmer for 1 hour, or until the chicken is tender and cooked through.
7. Taste and adjust the seasoning with salt and pepper if needed.
8. Serve the Chicken and Date Tagine hot, garnished with fresh cilantro. It pairs well with couscous or rice.

Nutrition information:
- Calories: 380
- Fat: 15g

- Carbohydrates: 35g
- Protein: 25g
- Fiber: 4g
- Sugar: 28g
- Sodium: 450mg

the cookbook, Tantalizing Tagines: 99 Exquisite Recipes for Tagine Cooking, is an exciting task. We have explored the history and unique flavors of Moroccan tagine cooking, along with tips for preparing this uncommon form of cooking. We have learned that tagines are a hearty and flavorful way to bring creativity to the table.

The recipes in this cookbook span all levels of skill and complexity, from beginner to advanced. They feature classic tagine dishes like couscous and lamb, as well as more adventurous options like pumpkin and chorizo tagines. No matter what experience you have in the kitchen, there is something here for everyone. All of the recipes are easy to follow with clear step-by-step instructions, and any ingredients that may not be easy to find are explained in detail.

Tagines make for a great center piece of any dinner party, or even just a special occasion meal for a cozy night in. By following the directions in the cookbook, you can learn to craft flavorful dishes that will tantalize the palates of your guests and family. You can even experiment with the recipes to create your own delicious creations.

Tagine cooking is an adventurous way to explore the flavors of Morocco. From spices to the tenderness of the meat, tagines have the potential to surprise and delight. Thanks to this cookbook, you will now have a greater understanding of the ingredients used in tagines, and of the flavor combinations available to you. No matter whether you are a beginner or a seasoned pro, you can create wonderful tagine dishes in the comfort of your own home.

In conclusion, Tantalizing Tagines: 99 Exquisite Recipes for Tagine Cooking is the perfect guide for anyone looking to take their skills in the kitchen to the next level. This cookbook encourages adventure and creativity, and provides the reader with all the information they need to whip up delicious and beautiful tagines no matter their skill level. With the help of this cookbook, you will be able to craft meals that will tantalize your guests, impress the family, and make your evenings even more special. We hope you enjoy your culinary journey into Moroccan cooking with the help of this delicious cookbook.

www.ingramcontent.com/pod-product-compliance
Ingram Content Group UK Ltd.
Pitfield, Milton Keynes, MK11 3LW, UK
UKHW021934200726
13853UKWH00011B/2042

9 798860 545953